Workbook

MW00453729

Entrepreneurship: Ideas in Action

FIFTH EDITION

Cynthia L. Greene

SOUTH-WESTERN
CENGAGE Learning

Australia • Brazil • Japan • Korea • Mexico • Singapore • Spain • United Kingdom • United States

For product information and technology assistance, contact us at **Cengage Learning Academic Resource Center, 1-800-423-0563**.

For permission to use material from this text or product, submit all requests online at **www.cengage.com/permissions**. Further permissions questions can be emailed to **permissionrequest@cengage.com**.

ISBN-13: 978-0-840-06486-8
ISBN-10: 0-840-06486-1

South-Western Cengage Learning
5191 Natorp Boulevard
Mason, OH 45040
USA

Cengage Learning is a leading provider of customized learning solutions with office locations around the globe, including Singapore, the United Kingdom, Australia, Mexico, Brazil, and Japan. Locate your local office at: **international.cengage.com/region**.

Cengage Learning products are represented in Canada by Nelson Education, Ltd.

For your course and learning solutions, visit **www.cengage.com**.

Purchase any of our products at your local college store or at our preferred online store **www.CengageBrain.com**.

Printed in the United States of America
4 5 6 7 8 9 10   20 19 18 17 16

Contents

1.1 All About Entrepreneurship

True or False

Directions   Place a *T* for True or an *F* for False in the Answers column to show whether each of the following statements is true or false.

Answers

1. Entrepreneurs try to meet the needs of the marketplace by supplying a product or service.   1. _____
2. Entrepreneurs and employees are both directly affected by the consequences of the decisions they make.   2. _____
3. Manufacturing businesses produce the products they sell.   3. _____
4. Entrepreneurial businesses include retailing businesses, such as clothing and furniture stores, but do not include service businesses.   4. _____
5. A travel agency is a retailing business.   5. _____
6. Entrepreneurs constantly change U.S. business and contribute to the nation's overall good.   6. _____
7. Small firms with fewer than 500 employees represent about 25 percent of all businesses in the United States today.   7. _____
8. The owner's business experience is a factor that contributes to the likelihood of success.   8. _____
9. Small businesses contribute billions of dollars to the U.S. economy every year.   9. _____
10. Small companies cannot take as many risks as large companies, so small companies are less likely to be innovative.   10. _____

Multiple Choice

Directions   In the Answers column, write the letter that represents the word, or group of words, that correctly completes the statement.

Answers

1. A person who takes the risk of a business venture is (a) not directly affected by his or her decisions, (b) an employee, (c) an entrepreneur, (d) sure to be successful.   1. _____
2. A person who works for someone else is (a) an entrepreneur, (b) an employee, (c) taking the risk of business venture, (d) the one who receives the profits of the business.   2. _____
3. Entrepreneurs try to (a) identify the needs of the marketplace, (b) meet the needs of the marketplace, (c) make a profit, (d) all of these.   3. _____
4. Manufacturing businesses (a) produce the products they sell, (b) sell products directly to consumers, (c) sell services, (d) take resources out of the ground.   4. _____
5. Which of the following is a retailing business? (a) Auto repair shop, (b) Grocery store, (c) Gold mine, (d) Farm.   5. _____
6. About how many new businesses do not survive beyond four years? (a) about half, (b) nearly one-quarter, (c) almost 90 percent, (d) about 10 percent.   6. _____
7. In U.S. history, entrepreneurs have (a) changed American business by developing unneeded products, (b) invented machines that decreased productivity, (c) been an important part of the American economy, (d) helped the American economy remain unchanged.   7. _____
8. Bernie Marcus and Arthur Blank (a) invented a harvesting machine, (b) founded Starbuck's Coffee Company, (c) opened the first Home Depot stores (d) cofounded an aircraft company.   8. _____
9. Major factors in a firm's success include (a) having adequate capital, (b) providing a product or service that meets customer needs, (c) the owner's reason for starting the firm in the first place, (d) all of these.   9. _____
10. In the United States today, small companies (a) can be more creative than large companies, (b) have innovating ideas that lead to technological change, (c) contribute billions of dollars every year to the U.S. economy, (d) all of these.   10. _____

Problem Solving

Directions   Answer the following questions in the space provided.

1. The first column of the following table lists what each of the six types of businesses does. Complete the table by identifying the type of business and providing three examples of the business.

	Type of Business	Examples
Sells products to people other than the final customer		
Sells services rather than products		
Generates fresh produce and other farm products		
Sells products directly to the people who use or consume them		
Takes resources out of the ground		
Produces the products it sells		

2. A consumer bought a pair of shoes at Heavenly Soles. The shoes were made by Sierra Shoes. Heavenly Soles purchased the shoes, which were part of a large shipment, from Hughes Apparel. Two years later, the consumer had the heels of the shoes repaired at Casey's Shoe Repair. Identify each of these businesses according to its type of entrepreneurial business.

Manufacturing business _____

Wholesaling business _____

Retailing business _____

Service business _____

Name _____ Class _____ Date _____

1.2 Is Entrepreneurship Right for You?

True or False

Directions   Place a *T* for True or an *F* for False in the Answers column to show whether each of the following statements is true or false.

Answers

1. Successful entrepreneurs need to be self-confident because they must make decisions alone, but they do not need to be creative because they can hire creative people.   1._____

2. Entrepreneurs need to be able to make quick decisions.   2._____

3. To determine if entrepreneurship is right for you, you need to perform a self-assessment   3._____

4. Everyone has the qualities and aptitude needed to become a successful entrepreneur.   4._____

5. Your past experiences are a key factor in determining your commitment to a business.   5._____

6. Aptitude is the ability to evaluate your strengths and weaknesses.   6._____

7. Before starting a business, it is important to identify the kinds of entrepreneurial opportunities that match your aptitudes and interests.   7._____

8. Entrepreneurship involves risk, which is both an advantage and a disadvantage.   8._____

9. An advantage of entrepreneurship is that owners make all decisions by themselves.   9._____

10. An advantage of entrepreneurship is that nobody tells an entrepreneur what to do.   10._____

Multiple Choice

Directions   In the Answers column, write the letter that represents the word, or group of words, that correctly completes the statement.

Answers

1. Which of the following is *not* a characteristic of a successful entrepreneur? (a) Determination, (b) Creativity, (c) Dependence, (d) Self-confidence.   1._____

2. Researchers have determined that successful entrepreneurs (a) want to make their own decisions, (b) do not always know what they want, (c) like to have someone else make decisions, (d) do not need to set goals.   2._____

3. Entrepreneurs must realize that there are other stakeholders in their businesses, such as (a) partners, (b) investors, (c) employees, (d) all of these.   3._____

4. Two key factors that aid an entrepreneur's commitment to a business are (a) hobbies and sales experience, (b) interests and past experiences, (c) interests and sales experience, (d) hobbies and athletic ability.   4._____

5. A self-assessment is an evaluation of your (a) hobbies and interests, (b) strengths and weaknesses, (c) past job experience, (d) ability to act quickly.   5._____

6. Aptitude is the ability to (a) act quickly, (b) evaluate interests, (c) learn a particular kind of job, (d) all of these.   6._____

7. To determine your suitability for entrepreneurship, you should assess your (a) strengths and weaknesses, (b) interests, (c) aptitude, (d) all of these.   7._____

8. An advantage of entrepreneurship is that entrepreneurs (a) can supervise others, (b) make all decisions themselves, (c) can work in a field that interests them, (d) do not need to set goals.   8._____

9. Risk is (a) an advantage of entrepreneurship, (b) a disadvantage of entrepreneurship, (c) neither a nor b, (d) both a and b.   9._____

10. A disadvantage of entrepreneurship is that entrepreneurs (a) do not have a regular income, (b) must implement creative ideas, (c) control their own destinies, (d) none of these.   10._____

Problem Solving

Directions   In the space below, list eight characteristics of successful entrepreneurs. For each, explain how a lack of the characteristic could contribute to the failure of a business.

1. _____
   _____
   _____
   _____

2. _____
   _____
   _____
   _____

3. _____
   _____
   _____
   _____

4. _____
   _____
   _____
   _____

5. _____
   _____
   _____
   _____

6. _____
   _____
   _____
   _____

7. _____
   _____
   _____
   _____

8. _____
   _____
   _____
   _____

1.3 Explore Ideas and Opportunities

True or False

Directions Place a *T* for True or an *F* for False in the Answers column to show whether each of the following statements is true or false.

Answers

1. Libraries have publications that provide data of interest to entrepreneurs. 1. _____
2. Many companies display their products at the Small Business Administration (SBA). 2. _____
3. You can learn about business opportunities by talking to other entrepreneurs. 3. _____
4. Assessing different business opportunities helps you identify those most likely to succeed. 4. _____
5. To decide whether or not a business opportunity is realistic for you, compare your background and experience with the experience of people who own that kind of business. 5. _____
6. It is not necessary to determine how much money it will take to start a business because you will be able to borrow the money you need. 6. _____
7. Financial goals may include how quickly you can pay your debts. 7. _____
8. Ideas are thoughts or concepts that come from creative thinking. 8. _____
9. Nonfinancial goals are only for entrepreneurs who are solely interested in financial gain. 9. _____
10. Your financial and nonfinancial goals do not have to be realistic. 10. _____

Multiple Choice

Directions In the Answers column, write the letter that represents the word, or group of words, that correctly completes the statement.

Answers

1. Possibilities from existing conditions are (a) ideas, (b) opportunities, (c) dreams, (d) goals. 1. _____
2. Business ideas can come from many different sources, such as (a) hobbies and interests, (b) past experiences, (c) inventions, (d) all of these. 2. _____
3. You can find out about business opportunities from (a) books and magazines, (b) government publications, (c) the SBA, (d) all of these. 3. _____
4. The SBA (a) holds trade shows, (b) publishes information that may be helpful for small businesses, (c) has a department in most public libraries, (d) buys products from entrepreneurs to help them make a profit. 4. _____
5. Special meetings where companies display their products are (a) trade shows, (b) entrepreneurial conventions, (c) job fairs, (d) poor places to learn about opportunities. 5. _____
6. All of the following can help you determine if a business opportunity is realistic *except* (a) the rate of business failure, (b) the market for that type of business, (c) the background needed to run that type of business, (d) the interest rates for loans at different banks. 6. _____
7. When comparing different business opportunities, an entrepreneur should (a) set financial goals, (b) set nonfinancial goals, (c) determine the hours needed to run the business, (d) perform a self-assessment. 7. _____
8. Financial goals can include (a) the best retirement age, (b) the monetary value of serving a community need, (c) how much money you will earn, (d) how many employees you will have in ten years. 8. _____
9. Nonfinancial goals are important for an entrepreneur because they (a) determine personal satisfaction, (b) increase sales, (c) guarantee success, (d) enable a business to earn a profit. 9. _____
10. Nonfinancial goals include all of the following *except* (a) serving a community need, (b) paying debts, (c) doing something you like, (d) enjoying personal independence. 10. _____

Problem Solving

Directions   Answer the following questions in the space provided.

1. What is the difference between an idea and an opportunity?

_____

_____

_____

_____

_____

_____

2. List three places where you can go to find information about business opportunities.

_____

_____

_____

3. For one of the places you listed in Question 2, describe the types of resources available.

_____

_____

_____

_____

_____

_____

_____

_____

4. How does comparing different business opportunities help you choose the one that will be the most successful for you?

_____

_____

_____

_____

_____

_____

5. Give three examples of a financial goal and three examples of a nonfinancial goal.

_____

_____

_____

_____

_____

_____

Entrepreneurship: Ideas in Action, 5e, Student Edition

1.4 Problem Solving for Entrepreneurs

True or False

Directions   Place a *T* for True or an *F* for False in the Answers column to show whether each of the following statements is true or false.

Answers

1. The best entrepreneurs use a formal problem-solving model to make decisions.   1. _____
2. Defining and quantifying the problem is the first step in the problem-solving process.   2. _____
3. Identifying one or two possible solutions is usually sufficient.   3. _____
4. Quantifying a problem helps a business owner determine how much it is worth to them to solve it.   4. _____
5. The problem-solving process is not complete until the action is evaluated.   5. _____
6. The fourth step in the problem-solving process is brainstorming.   6. _____
7. Communication and listening skills are vital to the problem-solving process.   7. _____
8. Brainstorming is always done in a group setting; it is a useless activity for an individual.   8. _____
9. Following a brainstorming session, a decision should be made immediately.   9. _____
10. Entrepreneurs should not be afraid of making mistakes.   10. _____

Multiple Choice

Directions   In the Answers column, write the letter that represents the word, or group of words, that correctly completes the statement.

Answers

1. Entrepreneurs may make effective decisions (a) alone, (b) by using a formal problem-solving model, (c) by using group problem-solving techniques, (d) all of these.   1. _____
2. A formal problem-solving model (a) consists of five steps, (b) is never necessary for everyday decisions, (c) is used only to gather information, (d) helps businesspeople solve problems in a logical manner.   2. _____
3. After the problem is defined and information gathered, you (a) try to quantify the problem, (b) identify various solutions, (c) make your decisions, (d) reach a consensus.   3. _____
4. In evaluating alternatives and selecting the best option, you (a) gather information about each alternative, (b) see if the selected alternative works, (c) decide how to implement the best option, (d) quantify or rank the alternatives.   4. _____
5. Which of the following is *not* a step in the decision-making process? (a) Identifying various solutions, (b) Taking action, (c) Evaluating the problem, (d) Gathering information.   5. _____
6. Brainstorming (a) involves discussing a large number of ideas, (b) is used to analyze practical ideas, (c) is a creative problem-solving technique, (d) none of these.   6. _____
7. Good communication is important in the problem-solving process because to solve problems, you will likely need to (a) interact with others, (b) request information and express your ideas, (c) listen to suggestions from others, (d) all of these.   7. _____
8. The final step in the problem-solving model is to (a) take action, (b) evaluate alternatives and select the best option, (c) evaluate the action taken, (d) identify solutions.   8. _____
9. In a brainstorming session, you should (a) write down only solutions that seem practical, (b) come up with as many ideas as possible, (c) evaluate each idea as soon as it is proposed, (d) always work with at least two other trusted colleagues.   9. _____
10. From an entrepreneur's perspective, mistakes (a) have no place in the problem-solving process, (b) will never be made if the problem-solving process is correctly followed, (c) can be a real learning experience, (d) are always a negative.   10. _____

Problem Solving

Directions Answer the following questions in the space provided.

1. List three places where you can find relevant information in the second step of the problem-solving model.

    _____

    _____

    _____

2. Select one of your answers to Question 1 and describe a situation in which the information obtained would be relevant.

    _____

    _____

    _____

    _____

    _____

3. The last step in the problem-solving model is evaluating the action. Explain what an entrepreneur could do if this evaluation showed that the action did not solve the problem.

    _____

    _____

    _____

    _____

    _____

4. Describe how brainstorming could be used in the problem-solving model.

    _____

    _____

    _____

    _____

5. Explain why good communication is important in the problem-solving process.

    _____

    _____

    _____

    _____

    _____

Entrepreneurship: Ideas in Action, 5e, Student Edition

Chapter 1 Assessment
Should You Become an Entrepreneur?

Vocabulary Review

Directions   In the Answers column, write the letter that represents the word, or group of words, that correctly completes the statement.

Answers

1. People who own, operate, and take the risk of a business

2. The process of running a business of one's own

3. People who work for someone else

4. Evaluation of your strengths and weaknesses

5. The ability to learn a particular kind of job

6. Special meetings at which companies display their products

7. Problem-solving technique that generates many fresh ideas

8. Possibilities that arise from existing conditions

9. Thoughts or concepts that come from creative thinking

a. aptitude
b. brainstorming
c. employees
d. entrepreneurs
e. entrepreneurship
f. ideas
g. opportunities
h. self-assessment
i. trade shows

1._____
2._____
3._____
4._____
5._____
6._____
7._____
8._____
9._____

Fill-in-the-Blank

Directions   For each item below, determine the word(s) that best complete the sentence. Write the word(s) in the Answers column.

Answers

1. Entrepreneurs try to identify the _____ of the marketplace.

1._____

2. _____ businesses sell products directly to the people who use or consume them.

2._____

3. If it is not possible to quantify the alternatives in the fourth step of the problem-solving model, the decision maker may _____ each alternative.

3._____

4. Successful entrepreneurs are _____-oriented.

4._____

5. To assess your suitability for entrepreneurship, you should consider your strengths, weaknesses, _____, interests, past experiences, and aptitude.

5._____

6. An advantage of entrepreneurship is that entrepreneurs are their own _____.

6._____

7. Analyzing _____ experiences and jobs can help you come up with ideas for a business you would enjoy owning.

7._____

8. In comparing different business opportunities, you should look at the particular _____ associated with the business.

8._____

9. How much money you want to earn is a(n) _____ goal.

9._____

10. The first step in the problem-solving model is to _____ the problem.

10._____

Problem Solving

Directions   Answer the following questions in the spaces provided.

1. For everything you do in life, you set goals. Goals help you stay on track and follow through with your plans. The best goals are SMART. SMART goals provide more direction for you.

   In the table below, define each component of a SMART goal. Then write a personal goal you have for yourself. Finally, rewrite your goal as a SMART goal.

SMART Goals	
SMART Goal Components	**Definition**
Specific	
Measurable	
Attainable	
Realistic	
Timely	
Goal	
SMART Goal	

2. For the SMART goal you have identified above, list at least five specific tasks that will help you achieve these goals and assign a deadline to each.

Task	Completion Date

Entrepreneurship: Ideas in Action, 5e, Student Edition

2.1 Entrepreneurs Satisfy Needs and Wants

True or False

Directions   Place a *T* for True or an *F* for False in the Answers column to show whether each of the following statements is true or false.

Answers

1. Needs are things that you must have in order to survive.   1._____

2. The role of business is to produce and distribute goods and services that people need and want.   2._____

3. The most basic of needs is security.   3._____

4. Both types of wants—economic and noneconomic—form the basis of an economy.   4._____

5. Needs and wants are unlimited.   5._____

6. Economic resources are not factors of production.   6._____

7. Services must be provided to you at the time you need them—they cannot be stored.   7._____

8. Human resources rarely perform specialized labor.   8._____

9. Natural resources are not limited in supply.   9._____

10. Capital resources include buildings and equipment.   10._____

Multiple Choice

Directions   In the Answers column, write the letter that represents the word, or group of words, that correctly completes the statement.

Answers

1. Needs include all of the following *except* (a) food, (b) video games, (c) basic clothing, (d) shelter.   1._____

2. Things that you think you must have in order to feel satisfied are called (a) needs, (b) preferences, (c) goals, (d) wants.   2._____

3. The psychologist who developed a theory on the hierarchy of needs was (a) Abraham Maslow, (b) Sigmund Freud, (c) Karl Jung, (d) Terrence McKenna.   3._____

4. According to the theory of hierarchy of needs, (a) everyone's needs will eventually be satisfied, (b) people must satisfy lower-level needs before focusing on higher-level needs, (c) everyone has the same needs, (d) needs and wants are usually the same.   4._____

5. Which need involves something that provides a sense of accomplishment, such as earning a college degree? (a) Esteem, (b) Social, (c) Self-actualization, (d) Security.   5._____

6. Products you can see and touch are called (a) services, (b) goods, (c) intangibles, (d) all of these.   6._____

7. The three types of economic resources an entrepreneur may use are called (a) factors of production (b) supply curves, (c) factors of consumption, (d) production hierarchies.   7._____

8. Raw materials supplied by nature are called (a) human resources, (b) capital resources, (c) natural resources, (d) monetary resources.   8._____

9. Which of the following would not be considered a capital resource? (a) Buildings, (b) Equipment, (c) The money needed to pay employees, (d) Employees.   9._____

10. In the U.S. economy, entrepreneurs (a) fulfill consumers' wants and needs, (b) provide employment, (c) help change the way people live, (d) all of these.   10._____

Problem Solving

Directions   Answer the following questions in the space provided.

1. In the following hierarchy of needs pyramid, correctly list each need and provide an example of each.

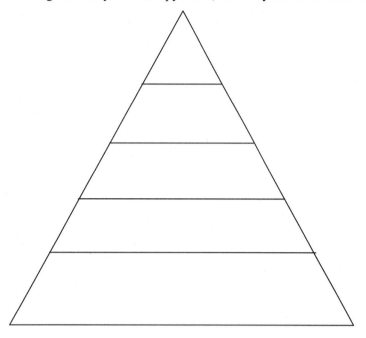

2. In the table below, list at least three needs from your own life. Then indicate where each ranks on the hierarchy of needs pyramid.

Need	Rank on Hierarchy

2.2 How Economic Decisions Are Made

True or False

Directions Place a *T* for True or an *F* for False in the Answers column to show whether each of the following statements is true or false.

Answers

1. Scarcity occurs when people's needs and wants are unlimited and the resources needed to produce the goods and services to meet those needs and wants are limited. 1._____

2. Opportunity cost is the cost of the last alternative. 2._____

3. The functions of business operate independently of each other. 3._____

4. A market economy is based on personal choice. 4._____

5. Traditional economies are used in developed countries. 5._____

6. A mixed economy often results when a country shifts away from a command economy toward a market economy but still has government involvement in the marketplace. 6._____

7. *Communism* is another name for the economic system in the United States. 7._____

8. The rivalry among businesses to sell their goods and services is called *competition*. 8._____

9. The value of the next-best economic alternative is the tradeoff cost. 9._____

10. A marketing mix is a combination of product, distribution, price, and promotion. 10._____

Multiple Choice

Directions In the Answers column, write the letter that represents the word, or group of words, that correctly completes the statement.

Answers

1. Scarcity exists because (a) there are different types of economies, (b) there are too many people in the world, (c) resources are limited, (d) some products are expensive to produce. 1._____

2. Scarcity occurs (a) only in command economies, (b) in every economy, (c) only in traditional economies, (d) only in mixed economies. 2._____

3. In a command economy, (a) there is very little choice in what is available, (b) people are not always able to obtain exactly what they want, (c) the government determines what products and services are produced, (d) all of these. 3._____

4. In a market economy, individual choice (a) does not influence how items are produced, (b) creates the market for a good or service, (c) has no effect on production, (d) creates scarcity. 4._____

5. Today, China operates under a (a) mixed economy, (b) traditional economy, (c) market economy, (d) command economy. 5._____

6. The U.S. economic system is based on all of the following principles *except* (a) private property, (b) freedom of choice, (c) government control, (d) competition. 6._____

7. All of these are a function of business except (a) production, (b) management (c) opportunity cost, (d) finance. 7._____

8. Competition performs all of the following functions in the U.S. economy *except* (a) it eliminates economic scarcity, (b) it forces businesses to improve products, (b) it helps keep the cost of products low, (d) it spurs businesses to provide good customer service. 8._____

9. All of the following are components of the marketing mix *except* (a) product, (b) distribution, (c) competition, (d) price. 9._____

10. Setting business goals would be considered primarily a function of (a) marketing, (b) production, (c) management, (d) finance. 10._____

Problem Solving

Directions   Answer the following questions in the space provided.

1. Explain the difference between a market economy and a command economy.

_____

_____

_____

_____

_____

_____

_____

2. Explain the four basic principles upon which the U.S. economy is based. Then tell which of these principles you think is the most distinctly "American." Explain your answer.

_____

_____

_____

_____

_____

_____

_____

_____

3. Identify at least three businesses in your community that are competitors. Then tell which of these businesses you prefer and why.

_____

_____

_____

_____

_____

_____

_____

Entrepreneurship: Ideas in Action, 5e, Student Edition

2.3 What Affects Price?

True or False

Directions   Place a *T* for True or an *F* for False in the Answers column to show whether each of the following statements is true or false.

Answers

1. The supply curve for a market economy shows that as the price of a good or service rises, suppliers are willing to produce more of the good or service.

   1._____

2. The demand curve for a market economy shows that as the price of a good or service rises, individuals are willing to consume more of the good or service.

   2._____

3. Demand elasticity occurs when demand for a product is affected by its price.

   3._____

4. Inelastic demand occurs when a change in price creates more demand.

   4._____

5. In a market with perfect competition, a small number of businesses gain the majority of total sales.

   5._____

6. When a company controls all of a market, it has a monopoly.

   6._____

7. Fixed costs must be paid even if a company has no sales.

   7._____

8. When the quantity of a good or service produced increases, variable costs remain the same.

   8._____

9. Marginal benefit measures the advantages of producing one additional unit of a good.

   9._____

10. It is difficult for new businesses to enter businesses in a market with an oligopoly market structure.

    10._____

Multiple Choice

Directions   In the Answers column, write the letter that represents the word, or group of words, that correctly completes the statement.

Answers

1. A supply curve shows that the quantity produced (a) increases as price decreases, (b) increases as price increases, (c) decreases as price increases, (d) is not affected by price.

   1._____

2. A demand curve shows that the quantity consumed (a) increases as price decreases, (b) increases as price increases, (c) decreases as price decreases, (d) is not affected by price.

   2._____

3. The forces of supply and demand determine (a) price in a market economy, (b) price in a command economy, (c) whether government controls prices, (d) none of these.

   3._____

4. At the equilibrium price, supply is (a) greater than demand, (b) at a minimum, (c) equal to demand, (d) at its highest point.

   4._____

5. In a competitive market, (a) there is no competition, (b) there is a monopoly, (c) supply will never equal demand, (d) buyers can shop around for the best deal.

   5._____

6. A company that controls all of a market (a) must compete for business, (b) cannot exist in a market economy, (c) has a monopoly, (d) has an oligopoly.

   6._____

7. When a market is dominated by a small number of businesses that gain the majority of total sales it is called (a) monopolistic competition, (b) pure competition, (c) its factors of production controlled by the government, (d) an oligopoly.

   7._____

8. The fixed costs of a business (a) include monthly rent, (b) are based on the price of supplies, (c) do not include the cost of insurance, (d) include advertising costs.

   8._____

9. If an entrepreneur's variable cost for each unit produced is $1.35, how much would the fixed costs increase if 30 additional units were demanded each day? (a) $40.50 per day, (b) $40.50 per week, (c) $202.50 per week, (d) none of these.

   9._____

10. When a business owner decides to grow the business he or she should consider the (a) equilibrium quantity, (b) variable cost, (c) marginal cost, (d) economies of scale.

    10._____

Problem Solving

Directions   Answer the following questions in the spaces provided.

1. Describe what a supply curve looks like.

   _____

   _____

   _____

   _____

   _____

2. Explain why a supply curve looks the way it does.

   _____

   _____

   _____

   _____

   _____

3. Describe what a demand curve looks like.

   _____

   _____

   _____

   _____

   _____

4. Explain why a demand curve looks the way it does.

   _____

   _____

   _____

   _____

   _____

5. What is the significance of the intersection point of the demand and supply curves for a product or service?

   _____

   _____

   _____

   _____

   _____

Entrepreneurship: Ideas in Action, 5e, Student Edition

Chapter 2 Assessment
Entrepreneurs in a Market Economy

Vocabulary Review

Directions In the space provided, write a sentence that correctly uses each of the following terms. Your sentence should *not* be a definition of the term.

1. equilibrium price

2. monopoly

3. variable costs

4. natural resources

Fill-in-the-Blank

Directions For each item below, determine the word(s) that best complete the sentence. Write the word(s) in the Answers column.

Answers

1. In a(n) _____ economy, the government allocates goods and services.

   1. _____

2. As the price of a good or service increases, _____ are willing to produce more.

   2. _____

3. As the price of a good or service decreases, _____ are willing to purchase more.

   3. _____

4. Marginal benefit measures the advantages of producing _____ additional unit of a good or service.

   4. _____

5. Entrepreneurs make business decisions based on the concepts of marginal benefit and _____ cost.

   5. _____

6. An entrepreneur who chooses one alternative over another is using the concept of _____ cost.

   6. _____

7. When a market is dominated by a small number of businesses that gain the majority of total sales revenue, it is called a(n) _____.

   7. _____

8. _____ are activities that are consumed as they are produced.

   8. _____

9. The people who create goods and services are called _____ resources.

   9. _____

10. A market with _____ competition consists of a very large number of businesses producing nearly identical products and has many buyers.

    10. _____

Problem Solving

Directions   Answer the following questions. Show your work and write your answers in the spaces provided.

1. At a price of $7.95 each, a nursery sells 60 one-gallon plants a day. The owner hopes to increase total revenue by changing the price of these plants. Find the total revenue for each price shown in the following table.

Price	Number Sold per Day	Total Revenue per Day
$6.95	70	
$7.49	65	
$7.95	60	
$8.49	55	

Should the nursery owner change the price of the plants? Explain your answer.

_____

_____

_____

_____

_____

2. The owner of a specialty delicatessen buys baskets, decorates and fills them with food items, and sells them as one of the products in the shop. The entrepreneur sells an average of 130 baskets a month. The basket supplier charges $0.50 per basket. The entrepreneur would like to reduce his variable costs and has found a basket supplier who will charge only $0.40 per basket. How much will the delicatessen owner save in a year by changing suppliers?

_____

_____

_____

_____

3. An entrepreneur makes a part used in the auto industry that he sells for $2.65 each. Yearly sales of this part have been 20,400 a year for the last three years. The customer has cut production and has reduced its purchase of these parts by 35 percent. How much yearly revenue will the entrepreneur lose as a result?

_____

_____

_____

_____

_____

3.1 Why a Business Plan Is Important

True or False

Directions   Place a *T* for True or an *F* for False in the Answers column to show whether each of the following statements is true or false.

Answers

1. A business plan provides financial information that shows how your business will earn a profit.

   1. _____

2. How a business will get and keep customers is not a part of a business plan.

   2. _____

3. A business plan does not give suppliers much confidence when it comes to extending credit.

   3. _____

4. Businesses must have a completely new products or services to convince investors that the idea is solid.

   4. _____

5. A good business plan includes sales projections for the short, medium, and long term and sets forth future business plans.

   5. _____

6. The backgrounds and experience of the people who will be running the business help lenders make financing decisions.

   6. _____

7. A business plan will not help you think about all the aspects of your business.

   7. _____

8. Writing a business plan can help you identify problems you might encounter in the future.

   8. _____

9. Lenders require a business plan before they will consider financing a business.

   9. _____

10. After your business is up and running, you will rarely use your business plan.

    10. _____

Multiple Choice

Directions   In the Answers column, write the letter that represents the word, or group of words, that correctly completes the statement.

Answers

1. A business plan should (a) identify target customers, (b) show how your business will earn a profit, (c) detail who will run your business, (d) all of these.

   1. _____

2. Before lenders will loan money to a new business, (a) they will want to interview all potential employees, (b) the new business must have at least two years' worth of work already lined up, (c) they need to be convinced that the people running the business have the necessary skills to succeed, (d) all of these.

   2. _____

3. A business plan explains how your product or service (a) will be produced, (b) will be sold, (c) is either new or better than existing products or services, (d) all of these.

   3. _____

4. Long-term sales projections are (a) for two to four years after start up, (b) for five years in the future, (c) for ten years in the future, (d) not included in a business plan.

   4. _____

5. Which of the following is *not* a purpose of a business plan? (a) To describe the backgrounds and experience of your suppliers, (b) To explain the idea behind your business, (c) To explain how you expect to achieve specific objectives, (d) To describe the backgrounds and experience of the people who will be running the business.

   5. _____

6. Before they will consider financing a business, lenders require (a) an organizational chart that lists all of your employees, (b) a business plan, (c) the history and background of your product, (d) all of these.

   6. _____

7. After it is completed, you can use your business plan to (a) help manage your business, (b) identify your product or service, (c) identify your target customer, (d) make short-term sales projections.

   7. _____

8. A business plan is important for all of the following reasons *except* (a) it helps you communicate your ideas to others, (b) it helps you decide what to sell, (c) it can help you secure financing for your business, (d) it makes you think about all aspects of your business.

   8. _____

Problem Solving

Directions Answer the following questions in the space provided.

1. Explain how the three purposes of a business plan apply to obtaining financing for a new business.

   _____

   _____

   _____

   _____

   _____

   _____

   _____

   _____

2. Explain how the three purposes of a business plan apply to starting a new business if the entrepreneur does not need financing.

   _____

   _____

   _____

   _____

   _____

   _____

   _____

   _____

   _____

3. Explain why a business plan is important for every new business.

   _____

   _____

   _____

   _____

   _____

   _____

   _____

   _____

Entrepreneurship: Ideas in Action, 5e, Student Edition

3.2 What Goes Into a Business Plan?

True or False

Directions   Place a *T* for True or an *F* for False in the Answers column to show whether each of the following statements is true or false.

Answers

1. All business plans have different purposes, so they do not all have the same basic elements. 1. _____
2. Describing how you came up with the idea for your business can help others understand how your business will operate. 2. _____
3. Writing a business plan can force entrepreneurs to think about their goals. 3. _____
4. A handwritten business plan is acceptable if it is neat, well organized, and inviting to read. 4. _____
5. Only corporations need to include a form of ownership section in a business plan. 5. _____
6. Copies of resumes help show that owners are qualified to manage a business. 6. _____
7. The marketing section of your business plan should describe the location of your business. 7. _____
8. A financial statement based on projected revenues is called an informal financial statement. 8. _____
9. The financial section of your business plan should state how much money you need to borrow and how much you are investing in the business. 9. _____
10. A brief explanation of why you are asking for a loan and what you plan to do with the money is called an executive summary. 10. _____

Multiple Choice

Directions   In the Answers column, write the letter that represents the word, or group of words, that correctly completes the statement.

Answers

1. The introduction section of a business plan contains all of the following *except* (a) a description of the business and its goals, (b) the legal structure of the business, (c) an identification of risks, (d) the advantages your business has over your competitors. 1. _____
2. Information about necessary equipment for your business is included in the (a) financial management section, (b) concluding statement, (c) marketing section, (d) operations section. 2. _____
3. Your business plan should describe the location of your business because (a) different forms of ownership have different types of locations, (b) every industry has an ideal type of location, (c) location is often a critical factor in a business's success, (d) all of these. 3. _____
4. The marketing section of your plan explains (a) how you plan to enter the market, (b) who your prospective customers are, (c) your advantages over the competition, (d) all of these. 4. _____
5. In the financial management section, a new business must include (a) projected financial statements, (b) copies of all rental agreements, (c) current financial statements, (d) all of these. 5. _____
6. Which of the following is *not* an element of the financial management section of your plan? (a) Identification of risks, (b) Distribution of profits and losses, (c) Financial statements, (d) Funding request and return on investment. 6. _____
7. A letter that introduces and explains an accompanying document is called a(n) (a) cover letter, (b) introductory letter, (c) statement of purpose, (d) letter of intent. 7. _____
8. An executive summary (a) should be written before the business plan is completed, (b) includes supporting documents that back up statements made in the body of the report, (c) state the amount you want to borrow, (d) must never be longer than two paragraphs. 8. _____
9. A business plan's title page includes all of the following *except* (a) a summary of the plan, (b) the name of your company, (c) the date, (d) the owner's name. 9. _____
10. The appendix of a business plan might include (a) tax returns of the business owner, (b) letters of recommendation, (c) a copy of required licenses, (d) all of these. 10. _____

Problem Solving

Directions   Answer the following questions in the space provided.

1. In the marketing section of your business plan, you need to provide information in four areas.

    a. What information should be included about your products or services?

    _____

    _____

    _____

    _____

    b. What information should be included about your market?

    _____

    _____

    _____

    _____

    c. What information should be included about the industry you will operate in?

    _____

    _____

    _____

    _____

    d. How might the location of your business affect its success?

    _____

    _____

    _____

    _____

2. The financial management section of your business plan consists of three elements. List these elements, describe what is included in each, and explain why the information is necessary.

    _____

    _____

    _____

    _____

    _____

    _____

    _____

    _____

    _____

3.3 How to Create an Effective Business Plan

True or False

Directions Place a *T* for True or an *F* for False in the Answers column to show whether each of the following statements is true or false.

Answers

1. To convince readers that you have a practical business plan, you must include information and data from objective sources.

   1. _____

2. Writing an effective business plan should only take 24 hours.

   2. _____

3. Counselors from Small Business Development Centers and volunteers from SCORE can provide advice and workshops to help you develop your business plan.

   3. _____

4. Entrepreneurs can hire experts from trade associations to help them prepare business plans.

   4. _____

5. The Internet is not a trusted source of information on how to develop a business plan.

   5. _____

6. A local Chamber of Commerce can provide information on trends affecting local businesses, local resources, and zoning and licensing information.

   6. _____

7. Entrepreneurs should avoid seeking advice from bankers or accountants because doing so will make them appear inexperienced and unqualified to run a business.

   7. _____

8. An undefined target market can ruin a business plan.

   8. _____

9. Never reveal your competitors' strengths in your business plan—focus only on what they are doing wrong.

   9. _____

10. The only person who should read a business plan is the owner and potential investors.

    10. _____

Multiple Choice

Directions In the Answers column, write the letter that represents the word, or group of words, that correctly completes the statement.

Answers

1. Assistance from an SBDC is available to (a) anyone who cannot afford the services of a private consultant, (b) existing business owners only, (c) first-time business owners only, (d) minority business owners only.

   1. _____

2. The retired executives at SCORE (a) provide advice for a small fee, (b) hold inexpensive workshops, (c) represent all areas of business, (d) have offices at the SBA.

   2. _____

3. Which of the following is an independent agency of the federal government that helps Americans start, build, and grow businesses? (a) SCORE, (b) the SBA, (c) local Chambers of Commerce, (d) all of these.

   3. _____

4. Trade associations provide all of the following to entrepreneurs *except* (a) useful information, (b) education, (c) networking opportunities, (d) small loans.

   4. _____

5. Which of the following is *least* likely to be a helpful resource for your business plan? (a) *National Geographic*, (b) books on entrepreneurship, (c) SBA publications, (d) *BusinessWeek* magazine.

   5. _____

6. Online business resources (a) should not be used in a business plan, (b) are not as reliable as print resources, (c) can be found via search engines, (d) are not available from the SBA.

   6. _____

7. Financial projections in a business plan should be (a) left out of your business plan if you could not locate reliable financial information, (b) based on solid evidence, (c) very optimistic, in order to impress investors, (d) based on your best guess.

   7. _____

8. Your business plan must (a) clearly define your market, (b) never overlook the competition, (c) be consistent, (d) all of these.

   8. _____

Problem Solving

Directions   Answer the following questions in the space provided.

1. List five organizations that can be used as resources to obtain information or assistance for preparing a business plan.

   _____

   _____

   _____

   _____

   _____

   _____

2. Describe the types of print resources that are available to help you research a business plan and where you can obtain them.

   _____

   _____

   _____

   _____

   _____

3. Describe the types of online resources that are available to help you research a business plan.

   _____

   _____

   _____

   _____

4. Describe the people resources that are available to help you research a business plan and the type of information each provides.

   _____

   _____

   _____

   _____

   _____

5. Describe any additional resources that can help you research a business plan and the type of information each provides.

   _____

   _____

   _____

   _____

   _____

Chapter 3 Assessment
Develop a Business Plan

Vocabulary Review

Directions   In each of the following sentences, the underlined term is not used correctly. In the space provided, rewrite the sentence so the term is used correctly.

1. A business plan is a handwritten document that lists all the steps necessary in operating a business.

2. In the history and background section of a business plan, an entrepreneur should include pro forma financial statements, which are statements of the funding request and return on investment.

3. Trade associations are organizations of retired executives and can be valuable sources of information in researching a business plan.

Fill-in-the-Blank

Directions   For each item below, determine the word(s) that best complete the sentence. Write the word(s) in the Answers column.

Answers

1. Medium-term sales objectives cover a period of about _____ years.
1._____

2. A business plan may help you secure _____ for your business.
2._____

3. A description of the industry in which you will operate your business is found in the _____ section of a business plan.
3._____

4. The _____ section of a business plan discusses hiring procedures.
4._____

5. A common mistake made by many entrepreneurs is to provide _____ financial projections in their business plans.
5._____

6. In many communities, the local Chamber of _____ offers assistance and information to entrepreneurs.
6._____

7. The retired executives who volunteer with _____ provide free confidential advice that can help entrepreneurs prepare their business plans.
7._____

8. The cover letter for your business plan should briefly describe your business and its potential for success and tell how much _____ you need.
8._____

9. A business plan must provide detailed financial information that shows how your business will succeed in earning a _____.
9._____

10. In the concluding statement of a business plan, you should emphasize your commitment to the _____ of the business.
10._____

Problem Solving

Directions Answer the following questions. Write your answers in the spaces provided.

1. In the first column of the following table, list the introductory elements of a business plan in the order in which they should appear. In the second column, describe the physical characteristics of each element, such as length, format, and so on. In the third column, describe what the element should include. The first element is listed as an example.

Introductory Element	Physical Characteristics	Contents

2. Describe what should be included in the appendix of a business plan.

_____

_____

_____

_____

_____

Entrepreneurship: Ideas in Action, 5e, Student Edition

4.1 Identify Your Market

True or False

Directions   Place a *T* for True or an *F* for False in the Answers column to show whether each of the following statements is true or false.

Answers

1. Entrepreneurs estimate demand for their products and services by identifying their target market.

   1. _____

2. Understanding your customers allows you meet customer demands.

   2. _____

3. Demographics describe a group of people in terms of their tastes, opinions, personality traits, and lifestyle habits.

   3. _____

4. Marital status, family size, and age are useful data for identifying your target market.

   4. _____

5. A customer profile should include demographic data but not psychographic data.

   5. _____

6. Segmenting your target market is usually not necessary because most markets are small.

   6. _____

7. Data that helps you determine how often potential customers use a particular service is called a customer profile.

   7. _____

8. A market segment is made up of people with common characteristics.

   8. _____

9. Customers should never be profiled based geographic data.

   9. _____

10. A marketing strategy identifies customers that you can better serve than your competitors, but it cannot help you determine the *size* of your market.

    10. _____

Multiple Choice

Directions   In the Answers column, write the letter that represents the word, or group of words, that correctly completes the statement.

Answers

1. The customers you would most like to attract are referred to as your (a) competition, (b) market segments, (c) target market, (d) demographics.

   1. _____

2. Demographics are data that describe a group of people in terms of their (a) income, (b) tastes, (c) opinions, (d) needs.

   2. _____

3. Psychographics are data that describe a group of people in terms of their (a) lifestyle habits, (b) personality traits, (c) opinions, (d) all of these.

   3. _____

4. By continually evaluating your market, you can respond to changes in all of the following *except* (a) government, (b) communities, (c) consumer tastes, (d) competitors' offerings.

   4. _____

5. A description of the characteristics of the person or company that is likely to purchase a product or service is a (a) target market, (b) customer profile, (c) psychographic profile, (d) demographic summary

   5. _____

6. Most products and services appeal to (a) a large number of people, (b) the demographic market, (c) a market segment, (d) none of these.

   6. _____

7. Data that helps you determine how often potential customers use a particular service is called (a) a customer profile, (b) demographic data, (c) psychographic data, (d) use-based data.

   7. _____

8. Data that helps you determine where your potential customers live and how far they will travel to do business with you is called (a) use-based data, (b) geographic data, (c) census data, (d) secondary data.

   8. _____

Problem Solving

Directions   Answer the following questions in the space provided.

1. Describe the difference between demographic data and psychographic data.

_____

_____

_____

_____

_____

2. How do demographic and psychographic data relate to identifying your target market?

_____

_____

_____

_____

3. An entrepreneur developed the customer profile for her pet store. Which of the information in the profile is demographic data? Which of the information is psychographic data? Which of the information is geographic data?

CUSTOMER PROFILE FOR A PET STORE
• Individual or couple 25 to 55 years of age
• Own one or more pets
• One or both members of household work full time in professional field
• Want high-quality pet foods and accessories
• Willing to pay high prices for high quality
• Live in exclusive city residential area
• Average household income: $135,000

_____

_____

_____

_____

_____

_____

_____

4. List ten market segments for the retail clothing market.

_____

_____

_____

_____

_____

_____

4.2 Research the Market

True or False

Directions   Place a *T* for True or an *F* for False in the Answers column to show whether each of the following statements is true or false.

Answers

1. To gather information for market research, you can use either secondary data or primary data but not both.   1._____

2. Information collected for the very first time to fit a specific purpose is primary data.   2._____

3. Focus groups are quick interviews with target customers.   3._____

4. The first step in primary market research is to select a research method.   4._____

5. Collecting primary data can be expensive and time-consuming.   5._____

6. Secondary data are found in already published sources.   6._____

7. Observation is the best research method if you want to find out people's opinions.   7._____

8. Economic trends and industry forecasts help determine the kind of primary data research to perform.   8._____

9. A survey question should not be included if the response serves no specific purpose.   9._____

10. You will not need to use your market research information until after you have developed a plan of action.   10._____

Multiple Choice

Directions   In the Answers column, write the letter that represents the word, or group of words, that correctly completes the statement.

Answers

1. Secondary data are found (a) in government publications, (b) on the Internet, (c) in newspapers, (d) all of these.   1._____

2. Which of the following is *not* a way to collect primary data? (a) Focus groups, (b) Consumer opinion blogs, (c) Surveys, (d) Observation.   2._____

3. The data collected in a telephone survey are (a) secondary data, (b) primary data, (c) population data, (d) computer data.   3._____

4. Finding hidden patterns and relationships in customer data is called (a) data warehousing, (b) data collection, (c) data mining (d) data evaluation.   4._____

5. Touch points are areas where a customer (a) likes a particular product, (b) might have contact with a company, (c) enjoys shopping in a mall, (d) will try a new service.   5._____

6. Customer relationship management (a) focuses on understanding customers as individuals (b) focuses on understanding customers as groups, (c) provides demographic and psychographic data, (d) none of these.   6._____

7. In designing a survey, you should consider all of the following *except* (a) length of the survey, (b) how you plan to administer it, (c) when you can get the best information, (d) the purpose of each question.   7._____

8. A good questionnaire should (a) have easy-to-answer questions, (b) be at least two pages long, (c) help you find suppliers, (d) explain in detail why you are conducting the survey.   8._____

Problem Solving

Directions   The three primary data research methods are listed below. For each, give a brief description of the method, explain the situation in which it would be used, and list some advantages and disadvantages of the method. Write your answers in the space provided.

1. Survey or questionnaire

_____

_____

_____

_____

_____

_____

_____

_____

_____

_____

2. Observation

_____

_____

_____

_____

_____

_____

_____

_____

_____

_____

_____

3. Focus group

_____

_____

_____

_____

_____

_____

_____

_____

_____

_____

4.3 Know Your Competition

True or False

Directions   Place a *T* for True or an *F* for False in the Answers column to show whether each of the following statements is true or false.

Answers

1. An opportunity for success exists when a customer need is being unmet by a competitor.   1._____

2. To convince customers to buy from you instead of your competition, you need information about your competitors.   2._____

3. Secondary data resources and observation can help you learn about your direct competitors.   3._____

4. Your indirect competitors are those businesses that make most of their money selling products or services that are the same as or similar to yours.   4._____

5. One reason why small entrepreneurs can compete successfully with large retailers is because large retail chains carry more than one product line.   5._____

6. Large businesses often drive out smaller businesses by offering lower prices and more jobs.   6._____

7. Analyzing the strengths and weaknesses of your competition is a waste of resources.   7._____

8. Your analysis of competitors should include their prices, locations, and facilities.   8._____

9. A few customer complaints are not important if your business has a better location and better prices than your competition.   9._____

10. Superior service, easy return policies, and frequent-buyer programs are some of the strategies you can use to maintain customer loyalty.   10._____

Multiple Choice

Directions   In the Answers column, write the letter that represents the word, or group of words, that correctly completes the statement.

Answers

1. A small business selling specialty items will likely face __?__ from a large retailer. (a) demographic competition, (b) incidental competition, (c) indirect competition, (d) unfocused competition.   1._____

2. All of the following can provide information about direct competition *except* (a) the Postal Service, (b) the telephone directory, (c) the Chamber of Commerce, (d) observation methods.   2._____

3. As an entrepreneur, you may find that indirect competitors (a) are more difficult to locate than direct competitors, (b) are usually located in malls or shopping centers, (c) make most of their money selling the same product or service that you sell, (d) none of these.   3._____

4. Small businesses may have difficulty competing with large retailers because large retailers (a) develop more complete customer profiles, (b) can keep larger quantities of products in stock, (c) have a larger target market, (d) offer superior service.   4._____

5. Competitive analysis does all of the following *except* (a) list competitors, (b) summarize competitor products and prices, (c) identify threats from a competitor, (d) research a competitor's business plan.   5._____

6. Competitors should be analyzed concerning their (a) prices, (b) locations, (c) strengths and weaknesses, (d) all of these.   6._____

7. Customer feedback is considered a type of (a) problem solving, (b) market research, (c) target market, (d) customer profile.   7._____

8. All of the following are strategies designed to maintain customer loyalty *except* (a) providing store-specific credit cards, (b) locating in a city center, (c) listening to customers and responding to feedback, (d) having more convenient hours than other businesses.   8._____

Problem Solving

Directions   Answer the following questions in the space provided.

1. How might the competition in a rural area or small town be different than the competition in a large metropolitan area?

   _____

   _____

   _____

   _____

   _____

2. How does analyzing the strengths and weaknesses of specific competitors help an entrepreneur?

   _____

   _____

   _____

   _____

   _____

3. What might an entrepreneur do to compete with mail-order businesses that sell the same product?

   _____

   _____

   _____

   _____

   _____

   _____

4. What strategies can owners of small businesses use to compete with large retailers?

   _____

   _____

   _____

   _____

   _____

5. What is the most important way to maintain customer loyalty?

   _____

   _____

   _____

   _____

   _____

Chapter 4 Assessment
Identify and Meet a Market Need

Vocabulary Review

Directions In the space provided, write a sentence that correctly uses each of the following terms. Your sentence should *not* be a definition of the term.

1. demographics

2. secondary data

3. focus group

4. direct competition

Fill-in-the-Blank

Directions For each item below, determine the word(s) that best complete the sentence. Write the word(s) in the Answers column.

Answers

1. Identifying your _____ market helps you to reach the people you most want to sell to.

1. _____

2. Without _____, companies cannot remain in business.

2. _____

3. Part of understanding your customers is knowing their demographics and _____.

3. _____

4. A description of the characteristics of the person or company that is likely to purchase a product or service is a(n) _____.

4. _____

5. Market _____ are groups of customers that share common characteristics.

5. _____

6. An opportunity exists for an entrepreneur when a customer need is going unmet by a(n) _____.

6. _____

7. Information collected for the first time by observation or surveys is _____ data.

7. _____

8. A questionnaire or _____ can be read over the phone or mailed to respondents.

8. _____

9. The last step in the market research process is _____.

9. _____

10. Competition by a business that makes only a small amount of money selling the same or similar products or services as another business is _____ competition.

10. _____

Problem Solving

Directions   Answer the following questions in the space provided.

1. List at least six questions an entrepreneur needs to answer in order to identify the target market for his/her product or service.

_____

_____

_____

_____

_____

_____

_____

_____

2. Describe the types of demographic and psychographic data that are available in secondary data resources and that can be useful in market research.

_____

_____

_____

_____

_____

_____

_____

_____

_____

3. In the table below, identify a business you patronize frequently. Then list all of the direct competitors of this business you can think of—local, national, or online.

Business You Patronize	Direct Competitors

5.1 Develop the Marketing Plan

True or False

Directions   Place a *T* for True or an *F* for False in the Answers column to show whether each of the following statements is true or false.

Answers

1. A marketing mix is the blending of product, distribution, price, and promotion to satisfy a target market.

    1. _____

2. Establishing short-, medium-, and long-term marketing goals ensures that the marketing you do today fits the vision you have for your business tomorrow.

    2. _____

3. Long-term goals are what you want your business to achieve in the next two or three years.

    3. _____

4. Short-term goals should not be listed in terms of product price, distribution, and promotion.

    4. _____

5. Medium-term goals are used to create strategies for each element of the marketing mix.

    5. _____

6. If a short-term goal is to generate traffic in a retail store, the marketing strategy should focus on the market share of the competition.

    6. _____

7. Long-term goals show where you would like your business to be five or ten years from now but do not help you think about how to market your business today.

    7. _____

8. A written marketing plan can help you define your market and identify your customers.

    8. _____

9. The marketing concept uses the needs of entrepreneurs as the primary focus during the planning, production, distribution, and promotion of a product or service.

    9. _____

10. Researching industry norms and past performances will help you develop appropriate performance standards for your marketing plan.

    10. _____

Multiple Choice

Directions   In the Answers column, write the letter that represents the word, or group of words, that correctly completes the statement.

Answers

1. Price is one of the elements of (a) the competition, (b) the marketing mix, (c) the channel of distribution, (d) market research.

    1. _____

2. To use the marketing concept, businesses must do all of the following *except* (a) identify what will satisfy customers' needs and wants, (b) operate profitably, (c) devote half of its profits toward marketing, (d) develop products that are better than other choices.

    2. _____

3. Marketing goals (a) need to be established only for the long-term, (b) help shape your marketing plan, (c) should never change, (d) can be used to determine your product mix.

    3. _____

4. Short-term goals can be stated in terms of (a) number of customers, (b) level of profits, (c) level of sales, (d) all of these.

    4. _____

5. Your marketing strategy should address (a) product introduction or innovation, (b) pricing, (c) market share, (d) all of these.

    5. _____

6. Medium-term goals describe what you want your business to achieve (a) in ten years, (b) in terms of market share, (c) in two to five years, (d) by using various promotion methods.

    6. _____

7. A long-term goal might be to (a) expand by adding a second location, (b) increase market share to 50 percent, (c) establish a customer base, (d) network with local lawyers, accountants, and other business owners.

    7. _____

8. A marketing plan should do all of the following *except* (a) identify your overall market strategy, (b) include your specific strategies for price, product, distribution, and promotion, (c) identify the owner's net worth, (d) identify and anticipate change.

    8. _____

Problem Solving

Directions   Answer the following questions in the space provided.

1. Explain the difference between short-term, medium-term, and long-term goals for your business and short-term, medium-term, and long-term marketing goals.

_____

_____

_____

_____

_____

_____

_____

2. How can elements of the marketing mix be used to develop short-term marketing strategies?

_____

_____

_____

_____

_____

_____

_____

3. Why does a business need a marketing plan?

_____

_____

_____

_____

_____

_____

4. What kinds of information must be included in a marketing plan?

_____

_____

_____

_____

_____

_____

5.2 The Marketing Mix—Product

True or False

Directions   Place a *T* for True or an *F* for False in the Answers column to show whether each
of the following statements is true or false.

Answers

1. The different products and services a business sells are its inventory.   1. _____

2. Product features include such things as color, size, quality, hours, warranties, delivery, and   2. _____
   installation.

3. Products in the same category, such as cars, are positioned in the market to serve different   3. _____
   customer needs.

4. The marketing concept is the belief that the wants and needs of customers are the most   4. _____
   important consideration when developing any product or marketing effort.

5. Since the 1960s, the U.S. market has changed from being a consumer-driven market to   5. _____
   being a product-driven market.

6. For many businesses, a small percentage of product selection often makes up the majority   6. _____
   of the sales revenue.

7. Not every product has features.   7. _____

8. The marketing concept can give small businesses an advantage over larger businesses.   8. _____

9. Branding is the name, symbol, or design used to identify your product.   9. _____

10. The product mix often includes items of convenience for customers, even though they are   10. _____
    not profitable.

Multiple Choice

Directions   In the Answers column, write the letter that represents the word, or group of words,
that correctly completes the statement.

Answers

1. A product mix (a) is the different products and services a business sells, (b) identifies   1. _____
   features such as color, size, and quality, (c) is used to maximize sales, (d) helps determine
   the pricing strategy.

2. To satisfy a specific customer need, a business (a) sets price objectives, (b) uses cost-based   2. _____
   pricing, (c) positions its product in a certain market, (d) uses channels of distribution.

3. The marketing concept is the belief that (a) large businesses have an advantage over small   3. _____
   businesses, (b) the wants and needs of customers are the most important consideration, (c)
   small businesses are less flexible when trying to satisfy customer needs, (d) all of these.

4. Product characteristics that will satisfy customer needs are called (a) brands, (b) services,   4. _____
   (c) the product mix, (d) features.

5. The Nike "swoosh" is an example of a product (a) label, (b) brand, (c) feature, (d) package.   5. _____

6. Creating an image for a product in the customer's mind is called (a) positioning,   6. _____
   (b) branding, (c) packaging, (d) distributing.

7. When a company offers different products and services within the same category, (a) it is   7. _____
   trying to serve different customer needs, (b) its position strategy has failed, (c) it has failed to
   take the competition into account, (d) it will be unable to make a profit.

8. Companies that use the marketing concept will (a) focus on product features more than on   8. _____
   consumer needs, (b) select a product mix that will most appeal to their target customers,
   (c) no longer care about product profitability, (d) all of these.

Problem Solving

Directions   Answer the following questions in the space provided.

1. Identify the item at right as a brand, package, or label. Explain your answer.

Nutrition Facts		
Serving Size 1 cup (227g)		
Servings Per Container about 4		
Amount per Serving		
Calories 120	Calories from Fat 20	
		% Daily Value*
Total Fat 2g		3%
Saturated Fat 1.5g		8%
Trans Fat 0g		
Cholesterol 10mg		3%
Sodium 150mg		6%
Total Carbohydrate 18g		6%
Dietary Fiber 3g		12%
Sugars 15g		
Protein 10g		
Vitamin A 0%	Vitamin C 0%	
Calcium 40%	Iron 0%	

*Percent Daily Values are based on a 2,000 calorie diet.

_____

_____

_____

_____

_____

_____

2. Name an automobile model that is positioned to satisfy customers' need for high quality and status. Then name an automobile model that is positioned to satisfy a need for inexpensive transportation. Describe the type of consumer who would buy each of the brands you name. Explain how the automakers of the models you have chosen use product features, branding, and positioning to make their products "stand out" from others and differentiate them in the marketplace.

3. Define the terms *product mix* and *positioning* and give an example of each for a retail bookstore.

5.3 The Marketing Mix—Price

True or False

Directions   Place a *T* for True or an *F* for False in the Answers column to show whether each of the following statements is true or false.

Answers

1. The *price* is the actual amount a customer pays for a product or service.   1._____

2. Return on investment is the amount earned as a result of the investment and is expressed in fractions.   2._____

3. To determine the market share of a business, the total market for a product must be known.   3._____

4. Your market share rarely depends on the level of competition in your market.   4._____

5. Businesses can increase market share by networking with potential customers.   5._____

6. With cost-based pricing, the price is determined by using the wholesale cost of an item as the basis for the price charged.   6._____

7. Demand-based pricing is used only by businesses that are monopolies.   7._____

8. With competition-based pricing, the price charged is the same as the price charged by competitors.   8._____

9. When services are combined under one price, rather than making the customer pay for each individual part of the service, this is called price skimming.   9._____

10. Price lining involves offering different levels of prices for a specific category of product based on features and quality.   10._____

Multiple Choice

Directions   In the Answers column, write the letter that represents the word, or group of words, that correctly completes the statement.

Answers

1. All of the following are price objectives *except* (a) increase profits, (b) minimize sales, (c) attract customers, (d) discourage competition.   1._____

2. Businesses should always set their prices (a) lower than their competitors' prices, (b) based on their product mix, (c) high enough to make a profit, (d) all of these.   2._____

3. The total market for a product must be known in order to determine (a) short-term marketing goals, (b) market share, (c) how to write a marketing plan, (d) medium-term goals.   3._____

4. Networking is (a) establishing informal ties with people who can help your business grow, (b) a way to increase market share, (c) attending gatherings that can give you good opportunities to meet potential customers, (d) all of these.   4._____

5. A business may set its prices for products or services using (a) competition-based pricing, (b) cost-based pricing, (c) demand-based pricing, (d) all of these.   5._____

6. With cost-based pricing, a price is determined by (a) finding out what competitors charge for the same item, (b) using the wholesale cost of an item, (c) how much customers are willing to pay, (d) analyzing customer need.   6._____

7. Which of the following pricing techniques is often used in the introductory stage of a product? (a) Penetration pricing, (b) Prestige pricing, (c) Trade discounts, (d) Markdown pricing.   7._____

8. If the terms of an invoice read "2/10, net 30," this means that (a) a 12 percent discount may be taken if the invoice is paid within 30 days, (b) a 2 percent discount may be taken if the invoice is paid within 10 days, (c) one-fifth of the invoice amount must be paid within 30 days, (d) none of these.   8._____

Problem Solving

Directions   Answer the following questions in the space provided.

1. What is market share? How is it determined? How can a business increase its market share?

_____

_____

_____

_____

_____

2. Explain how price is determined using each of the following methods:

Cost-based pricing

_____

_____

_____

_____

_____

Demand-based pricing

_____

_____

_____

_____

_____

Competition-based pricing

_____

_____

_____

_____

_____

3. What is psychological pricing? Identify two techniques used in psychological pricing.

_____

_____

_____

_____

_____

Chapter 5 Assessment
Market Your Business

Vocabulary Review

Directions   In the space provided, write a sentence that correctly uses each of the following terms. Your sentence should *not* be a definition of the term.

1. marketing concept

2. positioning

3. networking

4. return on investment

Fill-in-the-Blank

Directions   For each item below, determine the word(s) that best complete the sentence. Write the word(s) in the Answers column.

Answers

1. The four elements of the _____ mix are product, distribution, price, and promotion.

1._____

2. The _____ mix of a business is made up of the different products and services it sells.

2._____

3. When a business uses a set percentage to determine a retail price, it is using _____ pricing.

3._____

4. A(n) _____ price is a price determined by subtracting a percentage amount from the retail price of an item.

4._____

5. A(n) marketing _____ is a plan that identifies how your marketing goals will be achieved.

5._____

6. _____ offers customers a reduced price.

6._____

7. Product characteristics that will satisfy customer needs are called _____.

7._____

8. The _____ is the box, container, or wrapper in which the product is placed.

8._____

9. _____ is based on the belief that certain prices have an impact on how a customer perceives a product.

9._____

10. A business's market _____ will depend on the level of competition in its market.

10._____

Problem Solving

Directions Answer the following questions in the space provided.

1. List six questions that investors will expect your marketing plan to answer.

_____

_____

_____

_____

_____

_____

2. Marcos has invested $7,500 in his submarine sandwich shop near a local college. He wants to earn a 15 percent return on investment. How will his desired ROI impact Marcos' pricing strategy? How much will he need to earn to meet his goal?

_____

_____

_____

_____

_____

_____

3. Midori operates a sunglasses kiosk at a local mall. She buys a certain style of sunglasses for $12.50 a pair. To cover her operating expenses and allow for a profit, she adds 40 percent to her wholesale cost. What is the markup amount on the sunglasses? What is the retail price of the sunglasses? Show your work.

_____

_____

_____

_____

_____

_____

4. How does a business's product mix help to satisfy customers? Use your answer to explain why a bakery might offer several different varieties of bread.

_____

_____

_____

_____

_____

6.1 The Marketing Mix—Distribution

True or False

Directions   Place a *T* for True or an *F* for False in the Answers column to show whether each of the following statements is true or false.

Answers

1.   The routes that products take from the time they are produced until they arrive at a retail store are the channels of distribution.

1._____

2.   Retail stores can distribute their products to consumers by having convenient hours for customers, shipping directly to consumers, and being accessible through the Internet.

2._____

3.   Service businesses do not have a single, direct channel of distribution if there is more than one store in the chain.

3._____

4.   Direct distribution channels move products directly from the manufacturer to the consumer.

4._____

5.   Intermediaries are businesses that move products between manufacturers and consumers.

5._____

6.   No intermediaries are involved in the manufacturer to retailer to consumer channel option.

6._____

7.   Manufacturers usually don't sell directly to customers.

7._____

8.   A product may move through several channel members by various forms of transportation to get it to the point where it will ultimately be sold to consumers.

8._____

9.   If you are shipping a large item to another country, you would likely use the United States Postal Service.

9._____

10.   All types of businesses must receive goods from suppliers.

10._____

Multiple Choice

Directions   In the Answers column, write the letter that represents the word, or group of words, that correctly completes the statement.

Answers

1.   Channels of distribution include the routes that products and services take (a) from manufacturers to wholesalers, (b) from retail stores to consumers, (c) from manufacturers to retail stores, (d) all of these.

1._____

2.   Businesses need channels of distribution (a) for the products and services they sell, (b) only if they are manufacturers, (c) unless they buy directly from the manufacturer, (d) to market products on the Internet.

2._____

3.   Distributing a product or service on the Internet (a) is usually not cost-effective, (b) depends on how you create a web site, (c) may be a good idea for many businesses, (d) is too time-consuming for a small business.

3._____

4.   Intermediaries are used in (a) direct channels of distribution, (b) indirect channels of distribution, (c) the manufacturer-to-consumer channel option, (d) all of these.

4._____

5.   The most cost-effective channel option is (a) manufacturer-to-retailer-to-consumer, (b) manufacturer-to-consumer, (c) manufacturer-to-wholesaler-to-retailer-to-consumer, (d) consumer-to-retailer.

5._____

6.   Physical distribution includes all of the following except (a) branding, (b) transportation, (c) handling, (d) packaging of products.

6._____

7.   Storing products (a) typically reduces their cost, (b) eliminates the risk that they will be stolen, (c) helps balance supply and demand of products, (d) increases their shelf-life.

7._____

8.   You can find a listing of manufacturing companies in the United States in (a) *The American Wholesalers and Distributors Directory*, (b) *The Wall Street Journal*, (c) *The Thomas Register*, (d) your local Chamber of Commerce handbook.

8._____

Problem Solving

Directions   Answer the following questions in the space provided.

1. What are channels of distribution?

_____

_____

_____

_____

_____

_____

_____

2. List three different channels of distribution for a dishwasher manufacturer.

_____

_____

_____

_____

_____

_____

_____

_____

3. Where can you find information about distributors, wholesalers, and manufacturers for a retail business?

_____

_____

_____

_____

_____

4. Describe some of the benefits gained by both manufacturers and consumers when an intermediary is used in a channel of distribution. Give a real-world example with your answer.

_____

_____

_____

_____

_____

_____

Name _____ Class _____ Date _____

6.2 The Marketing Mix—Promotion

True or False

Directions Place a *T* for True or an *F* for False in the Answers column to show whether each of the following statements is true or false.

Answers

1. In choosing an advertising medium, cost is the most important factor. 1._____

2. The promotional mix usually involves one specific form of product promotion. 2._____

3. Online advertising is a cost-effective way for businesses to reach potential customers. 3._____

4. Although television advertising is very effective, it is expensive and generally reaches too broad an audience for most businesses. 4._____

5. A radio station will provide a psychographic profile of its listeners so that businesses can be sure they reach their target market. 5._____

6. Newspaper advertising is good for small firms because it targets a limited geographic area. 6._____

7. An advantage of advertising in a telephone directory is that people look there for a particular type of business. 7._____

8. Direct-mail advertising is effective only if people read it. 8._____

9. Although publicity is free, it can be negative if the media coverage is unfavorable. 9._____

10. A press release is a statement issued by the media to inform the public of an event. 10._____

Multiple Choice

Directions In the Answers column, write the letter that represents the word, or group of words, that correctly completes the statement.

Answers

1. A paid form of communication sent out by a business about a product or service is (a) publicity, (b) sales promotion, (c) advertising, (d) a press release. 1._____

2. In choosing an advertising medium, you should (a) always get advice from an advertising agency, (b) consider its effectiveness in reaching your target market, (c) decide whether to use a commercial or a paid advertisement, (d) distribute flyers in your area. 2._____

3. An online ad that changes the background of the page being viewed is called a (a) pop-up ad, (b) wallpaper ad, (c) banner ad, (d) floating ad. 3._____

4. Transit advertising consists of signs on (a) buildings, (b) semi-tractor trailers, (c) public transportation, (d) private automobiles. 4._____

5. A disadvantage of radio advertising is that (a) it is only an audio message, (b) radio stations tend to attract a particular kind of listener, (c) it is very expensive, (d) it reaches too broad an audience to be effective. 5._____

6. Newspaper advertising is good for small businesses because (a) it reaches too many people, (b) it targets a limited geographic area, (c) an advertisement competes with many others, (d) it is the largest form of advertising in the United States. 6._____

7. The main advantage of direct-mail advertising is that (a) the same advertisement can be used in a telephone directory, (b) most people read items sent through the mail, (c) mailing lists for target markets are available for purchase, (d) none of these. 7._____

8. Publicity is free promotion that (a) is generated by media coverage, (b) may involve staging an event or bringing in a celebrity, (c) may be favorable or unfavorable, (d) all of these. 8._____

Problem Solving

Directions Complete the following table by naming one advantage and one disadvantage of each of the forms of advertising listed.

Type of Advertising	Advantage	Disadvantage
Online		
Television		
Radio		
Newspaper		
Telephone directory		
Direct mail		
Magazine		
Outdoor		
Transit		

6.3 Selling and Promoting

True or False

Directions   Place a *T* for True or an *F* for False in the Answers column to show whether each of the following statements is true or false.

Answers

1. Entrepreneurs will need personal selling skills only if they are going into sales.

   1._____

2. A salesperson is often the only representative of the company the customers ever come in contact with.

   2._____

3. Personal selling is direct communication between a prospective buyer and a sales representative in which the sales representative attempts to influence the prospective buyer in a purchase situation.

   3._____

4. Benefits are the physical characteristics or capabilities of the product or service.

   4._____

5. Customers will usually always need the aid of a salesperson when making lower-level needs purchases.

   5._____

6. When customers know exactly what they want, the fulfillment of their needs is referred to as need satisfying.

   6._____

7. Satisfying a need is sometimes called problem resolution.

   7._____

8. Emotional buying decisions are based on the desire to have a specific product or service.

   8._____

9. Sales promotions are seldom sound business practices because discounts take away from profits.

   9._____

10. A coupon is a type of rebate.

   10._____

Multiple Choice

Directions   In the Answers column, write the letter that represents the word, or group of words, that correctly completes the statement.

Answers

1. A critical factor in the success of any business is (a) an entrepreneur's selling skills, (b) a large advertising budget, (c) making sure press releases are well written, (d) offering sales promotions at least once a month.

   1._____

2. Personal-selling skills become more important when customers (a) know exactly what they want, (b) try to satisfy their basic needs, (c), are making rational buying decisions, (d) seek to meet their upper-level needs.

   2._____

3. The physical characteristics or capabilities of a product or service are called (a) benefits, (b) features, (c) add-ons, (d) options.

   3._____

4. Using the phone to market your product is called (a) visual marketing, (b) telemarketing, (c) spam, (d) annoying.

   4._____

5. Which of the following is *not* a rational buying motive? (a) Safety, (b) Product quality, (c) Protection (d) Convenience.

   5._____

6. The first step in the consumer decision-making process is to (a) identify solutions, (b) define the problem, (c) gather information, (d) evaluate alternatives.

   6._____

7. Contests, coupons, free samples, and rebates are examples of (a) telemarketing, (b) sales promotion, (c) publicity, (d) advertising.

   7._____

8. The use of logos or signs to market your product or service is called (a) spamming, (b) junk calling, (c) phishing, (d) visual marketing.

   8._____

Problem Solving

Directions Answer the following questions in the space provided.

1. In the table below, identify three products you or your family recently purchased. List some features and benefits of each product. ***Student answers will vary; some examples are shown.***

Product	Features	Benefits

2. You are a salesperson in a mobile phone store. The brand-new Yakker 6800 Mobile Phone has the following features:

- Unique and Innovative Design
- High-Resolution Full-Color Display
- Compact Size
- Camera to Take Snapshots
- Synchronize Data by Linking Directly to Your PC
- Speed Dial for up to 9 Names

A customer has entered the store and is interested in the Yakker 6800. In the table below, associate each of the product features with a possible corresponding benefit for this customer.

Features	Benefits
Unique and Innovative Design	
High-Resolution Full-Color Display	
Compact Size	
Camera	
Links Directly to PC	
Speed Dial for up to 9 Names	

Entrepreneurship: Ideas in Action, 5e, Student Edition

Chapter 6 Assessment
Distribution, Promotion, and Selling

Vocabulary Review

Directions In the Answers column, write the letter that represents the word, or group of words, that correctly completes the statement.

Answers

1. Direct communication between a prospective buyer and a sales representative
2. Routes that products and services take from the time they are produced to the time they are consumed
3. A paid form of communication sent out by a business about a product or service
4. Uses intermediaries that move products between the manufacturer and the consumer
5. The act of establishing a favorable relationship with customers and the general public
6. Purchase decisions that are based on the logical reasoning of customers
7. A nonpaid form of communication that calls attention to your business through media coverage
8. Purchase decisions based on the desire to have a specific product or service
9. Moves the product directly from the manufacturer to the consumer

a. advertising
b. channels of distribution
c. direct channel
d. emotional buying decisions
e. indirect channel
f. personal selling
g. public relations
h. publicity
i. rational buying decisions

1. _____
2. _____
3. _____
4. _____
5. _____
6. _____
7. _____
8. _____
9. _____

Fill-in-the-Blank

Directions For each item below, determine the word(s) that best complete the sentence. Write the word(s) in the Answers column.

Answers

1. _____ is designed to protect the product from the time it is produced until it is consumed.
2. The strategy created by adopting a blend of advertising, publicity, personal selling, and sales promotion is called your _____ mix.
3. A _____ ad is a kind of online ad in which a new window opens in front of the current one, displaying an advertisement.
4. Billboards and signs are examples of _____ advertising.
5. Newspapers are the single largest medium of _____ in the United States.
6. _____ can be negative or positive depending on the media coverage.
7. In addition to advertising and publicity, a business can offer sales _____ as a way to increase sales.
8. Companies often offer a refund called a(n) _____ to customers who purchase their product.
9. Advantages that can result from features are called _____.
10. Giving away hats displaying your company name is an example of _____ promotion.

1. _____
2. _____
3. _____
4. _____
5. _____
6. _____
7. _____
8. _____
9. _____
10. _____

Problem Solving

Directions   Answer the following questions in the space provided.

1. You plan to start a dog-walking service in your community. You have prepared a thorough business plan, identified potential customers, and secured financing for your business. Now you are ready to get the word out to your target market. What kind of promotions will you use to get customers to patronize your new business?

_____

_____

_____

_____

_____

2. How can you determine the best method for transporting goods?

_____

_____

_____

_____

3. Use examples to explain how sales promotion can increase sales.

_____

_____

_____

_____

_____

4. Identify and describe the three most-common ways online advertising is purchased.

_____

_____

_____

_____

_____

_____

_____

_____

_____

Entrepreneurship: Ideas in Action, 5e, Student Edition

7.1 Decide to Purchase, Join, or Start a Business

True or False

Directions   Place a *T* for True or an *F* for False in the Answers column to show whether each of the following statements is true or false.

Answers

1. The owner of a business may sell the business because of insufficient sales or profits.   1._____

2. A business broker is a person who sells homes for a living.   2._____

3. A disadvantage of buying an existing business is that it may be poorly located.   3._____

4. When purchasing an existing business, you should find out why the business is being sold, inspect the facility, and analyze the financial accounts for the last three years.   4._____

5. A valuator can help determine a price to offer for a business and can write a sales contract.   5._____

6. A franchisee is a person who purchases a franchise agreement.   6._____

7. Advertising fees for franchises are paid directly to the advertisers.   7._____

8. The owner of a franchise must pay a weekly or monthly royalty fee to the seller of the franchise.   8._____

9. The Franchise Disclosure Document helps the franchise buyer to make a knowledgeable purchase.   9._____

10. Although recommended, it is not necessary to consult an attorney before purchasing a franchise.   10._____

Multiple Choice

Directions   In the Answers column, write the letter that represents the word, or group of words, that correctly completes the statement.

Answers

1. You can find businesses for sale through (a) classified ads, (b) leasing agents, (c) bankers, (d) all of these.   1._____

2. An advantage of buying an existing business is that (a) there will not be any customer goodwill, (b) suppliers are lined up, (c) it is making a profit, (d) less capital is required.   2._____

3. When buying an existing business, you should analyze financial accounting reports of operations for at least (a) one year, (b) two years, (c) three years, (d) none of these.   3._____

4. When buying a business, you should do all of the following *except* (a) meet with the seller, (b) inspect the business during working hours, (c) inspect a list of all customers, (d) have a lawyer draw up the sales contract.   4._____

5. The amount paid for the right to run a franchise is (a) an initial franchise fee, (b) a startup cost, (c) a royalty fee, (d) an advertising fee.   5._____

6. You should be suspicious when buying a franchise if the franchisor refuses to provide (a) written financial statements, (b) free advertising, (c) training or classes, (d) oral promises.   6._____

7. Franchisors may offer (a) to help finance the purchase, (b) to waive the royalty fees, (c) free nationwide advertising, (d) management and technical training.   7._____

8. Which of the following is *not* a disadvantage of working in a family business? (a) Family members hold key positions regardless of skills, (b) Family politics enter into decision-making, (c) The distinction between business life and private life is blurred, (d) The business benefits family members.   8._____

Problem Solving

Directions   Answer the following questions in the space provided.

1. Choose one advantage of buying an existing business and explain why it is an advantage.

    _____

    _____

    _____

    _____

    _____

2. Choose one disadvantage of buying an existing business and explain why it is a disadvantage.

    _____

    _____

    _____

    _____

3. What should you consider in addition to money when purchasing a franchise?

    _____

    _____

    _____

    _____

4. Which costs of purchasing a franchise would you still have if you start your own business?

    _____

    _____

    _____

    _____

5. Which costs of purchasing a franchise would *not* be incurred if you start your own business?

    _____

    _____

    _____

    _____

6. The franchise costs in Question 5 pay for benefits that reduce the risk of uncertainty in starting your own business. Explain why.

    _____

    _____

    _____

    _____

7.2 Choose a Legal Form of Business

True or False

Directions   Place a *T* for True or an *F* for False in the Answers column to show whether each
of the following statements is true or false.

Answers

1. A sole proprietorship enables two or more people to be in control of a business.   1._____

2. The government exercises very little control over sole proprietorships.   2._____

3. You must file a written description of your business with the government when you raise   3._____
    money for a sole proprietorship.

4. In a partnership, any losses will be shared by all the partners.   4._____

5. A partnership agreement should include a procedure for dealing with the death of a partner.   5._____

6. A partnership agreement identifies the investment contributed by each partner.   6._____

7. People who own shares of stock in a corporation are the owners of the corporation.   7._____

8. A corporation's senior officers decide how much should be paid out in dividends.   8._____

9. A corporation pays taxes both on its income and on the amount it pays out in dividends.   9._____

10. An S corporation's profits are taxed only as individual income, not as corporate income.   10._____

Multiple Choice

Directions   In the Answers column, write the letter that represents the word, or group of words,
that correctly completes the statement.

Answers

1. A business with the legal rights of a person and which may be owned by many people is a   1._____
    (a) sole proprietorship, (b) partnership, (c) corporation, (d) dual partnership.

2. A business is a sole proprietorship if (a) it is owned exclusively by one person, (b) it has   2._____
    fewer than ten employees, (c) it has the legal rights of a person, (d) all of these.

3. A disadvantage of a sole proprietorship is that (a) it must remain small, (b) it is difficult to   3._____
    start, (c) government regulation is extensive, (d) only the owner contributes money.

4. An advantage of a partnership is that (a) government regulations prevent disagreements,   4._____
    (b) decision making and responsibilities are shared, (c) it is easy to raise capital, (d) it has the
    legal rights of a person.

5. Which of the following is *not* included in a partnership agreement? (a) names of the partners,   5._____
    (b) conditions under which the partnership can be dissolved, (c) how dividends are to be
    distributed, (d) rights of each partner to review accounting documents.

6. In a corporation, each share of stock is (a) sold by a director of the company, (b) used to   6._____
    determine the amount of income tax, (c) a unit of ownership in the company, (d) a liability.

7. The board of directors of a corporation (a) sets up the company's accounting procedures,   7._____
    (b) determines the salaries of the senior officers, (c) pays dividends to shareholders, (d) may
    be held liable for all company debts.

8. The individual or group that owns the most shares of stock in a corporation (a) is liable for   8._____
    all corporate debts, (b) is called the board of shareholders, (c) receives all the profits,
    (d) maintains control of the company.

9. A limited liability company (a) cannot be formed by a single owner, (b) is not subject to the   9._____
    rules for an S corporation, (c) provides more tax benefits than an S corporation, (d) all of these.

10. The most common legal form of business in the United States is (a) sole proprietorship,   10._____
     (b) S corporation, (c) partnership, (d) limited liability company.

Problem Solving

Directions   Answer the following questions in the space provided.

1.   What are the advantages and disadvantages of a sole proprietorship?

_____

_____

_____

_____

2.   What are the advantages and disadvantages of a partnership?

_____

_____

_____

_____

3.   What are the advantages and disadvantages of a corporation?

_____

_____

_____

_____

4.   Suppose a company has debts of $120,000 when it goes out of business. Determine the liability in each of the following situations:

a. The company is a sole proprietorship.

_____

_____

_____

b. The company is a partnership with three partners. The partners have agreed to share profits and losses equally.

_____

_____

_____

c. The company is a corporation with 100 shares of stock worth $1,000 each. There are five shareholders; one owns 60 shares of stock and each of the other four owns 10 shares.

_____

_____

_____

7.3 Legal Issues and Business Ownership

True or False

Directions   Place a *T* for True or an *F* for False in the Answers column to show whether each of the following statements is true or false.

Answers

1. The Clayton Act makes it illegal for competitors to get together and set prices on the products or services they sell.   1._____

2. The Wheeler-Lea Act bans unfair or deceptive actions or practices by businesses.   2._____

3. The Antitrust Division of the FTC takes legal action against any business it believes has tried to monopolize an industry.   3._____

4. During the period a patent is in effect, no business or individual can copy or use the patented invention without permission from the patent holder.   4._____

5. Copyrights remain in effect for 20 years after the death of the author.   5._____

6. Regulations that protect consumers include trademarks, zoning regulations, and consumer protection laws.   6._____

7. The original, creative work of an artist or inventor is called intellectual property.   7._____

8. The Consumer Product Safety Act of 1972 sets safety standards for products other than food and drugs.   8._____

9. One of the most common reasons that a business hires a lawyer is to assist with contracts.   9._____

10. Consideration occurs when one party in a contract offers or agrees to do something and the other party accepts.   10._____

Multiple Choice

Directions   In the Answers column, write the letter that represents the word, or group of words, that correctly completes the statement.

Answers

1. The antitrust legislation that makes it illegal for competitors to set prices is the (a) Sherman Act, (b) Clayton Act, (c) Robinson-Patman Act, (d) Wheeler-Lea Act.   1._____

2. This law makes it illegal to charge different prices to different groups of nonretail consumers. (a) Sherman Act, (b) Clayton Act, (c) Robinson-Patman Act, (d) Wheeler-Lea Act.   2._____

3. The law that bans false or misleading advertising is the (a) Sherman Act, (b) Clayton Act, (c) Robinson-Patman Act, (d) Wheeler-Lea Act.   3._____

4. Laws that protect businesses involve (a) licenses, (b) zoning, (c) trademarks, (d) the Justice Department.   4._____

5. Restrictions on where businesses can locate are (a) licensing laws, (b) zoning laws, (c) consumer protection laws, (d) enforced by the FDA.   5._____

6. This law requires all banks to calculate credit costs in the same way. (a) Sherman Act, (b) Clayton Act, (c) Truth-in-Lending Act, (d) Fair Credit Billing Act.   6._____

7. The FTC monitors all of the following activities *except* (a) false or misleading advertising, (b) price setting by competitors, (c) price discrimination, (d) the sale of unhealthful foods.   7._____

8. This means the parties to a contract are legally able to enter into a binding agreement. (a) Consideration, (b) Legality, (c) Capacity, (d) Agreement.   8._____

9. You can learn about laws that affect your business (a) by reading books, (b) by taking a course in business law, (c) from the Internet, (d) all of these.   9._____

10. You may want to pay a lawyer to (a) help you hire employees with disabilities, (b) give you advice on insurance coverage, (c) discuss your prices with competitors, (d) none of these.   10._____

Problem Solving

Directions   The following table describes various laws that entrepreneurs should know and understand. Complete the table by identifying each law by name.

Description of Law	Name of Law
States that names, symbols, or special marks that distinguish certain businesses can be used only by the business.	
Sets safety standards for products other than food and drugs.	
States that it is illegal for a business to require a customer to purchase one good in order to be able to purchase another good.	
Regulations that control what types of buildings can be built in what areas.	
Helps consumers correct credit card billing errors.	
Makes it illegal for competitors to get together and set prices on the products or services they sell.	
Gives an inventor the sole right to produce, use, and sell an invention.	
Bans the sale of impure, improperly labeled, falsely guaranteed, and unhealthful foods, drugs, and cosmetics.	
Bans unfair or deceptive actions or practices by businesses.	
Establishes rights to exclusive publication, production, sale, or distribution of a literary or artistic work.	
Makes it illegal to charge different prices to different groups of nonretail customers.	

Chapter 7 Assessment
Select a Type of Ownership

Vocabulary Review

Directions   In the space provided, write a sentence that correctly uses each of the following terms. Your sentence should *not* be a definition of the term.

1. franchise

2. sole proprietorships

3. contract

4. intellectual property

Fill-in-the-Blank

Directions   For each item below, determine the word(s) that best complete the sentence. Write the word(s) in the Answers column.

Answers

1.   An advantage to buying an existing business is that it already has customers, _____, and procedures.

    1._____

2.   Before buying an existing business, you should analyze the _____ for at least the past three years.

    2._____

3.   The operating costs of a franchise include an initial franchise fee, _____, royalty fees, and advertising costs.

    3._____

4.   If a franchisee fails to make royalty payments, the franchisor can terminate the _____.

    4._____

5.   _____ are distributions of corporate profits to the shareholders.

    5._____

6.   The purpose of the _____ agreement is to set down in writing the rights and responsibilities of each of the owners.

    6._____

7.   Ownership of a(n) _____ is in the form of shares of stock.

    7._____

8.   Every corporation has a board of _____, which is a group of people who meet several times a year to make important decisions affecting the company.

    8._____

9.   A document that gives legal rights to inventors is a(n) _____.

    9._____

10.   Brand names may have a _____, which means that the name, symbol, or special mark can be used only by the business.

    10._____

Problem Solving

Directions Answer the following questions in the space provided.

1. The first column of the following table lists various criteria that entrepreneurs can use to assess business opportunities. Some criteria are based on characteristics of successful entrepreneurs; others are important considerations in business ownership. Rank from 1 to 4 the four types of entrepreneurial opportunities discussed in this chapter. A rank of 1 means the opportunity has the best chance of satisfying the criteria.

	Purchase an existing business	Enter a family business	Purchase a franchise	Start a business
Allows independence				
Requires setting challenging goals				
Encourages creativity				
Requires ability to make quick decisions				
High personal satisfaction				
Freedom to make decisions				
Low initial cost				
High initial profits				
High profit potential				
Easy to determine demand for product or service				
Normal working hours				
Low risk				
Easy to run initially				
Easy to acquire or start				
Easy to obtain financing				

2. Describe some conclusions you can draw from the table.

_____

_____

3. Do you think a person's strengths, weaknesses, and aptitudes influence the type of ownership chosen for a business? Explain your answer.

_____

_____

Entrepreneurship: Ideas in Action, 5e, Student Edition

8.1 Choose a Location

True or False

Directions   Place a *T* for True or an *F* for False in the Answers column to show whether each
of the following statements is true or false.

Answers

1. In choosing location you should be able to identify your trade area on a map.   1._____

2. Community shopping centers are small centers that serve specific neighborhoods.   2._____

3. Stand-alone stores must have a lot of parking because they often depend on drive-by traffic.   3._____

4. Warehouses are generally one of the most expensive rental facilities for a retail business.   4._____

5. For a travel agency or hair salon, location is less important than for a retail business.   5._____

6. Wholesale companies need a location that attracts a lot of retail traffic.   6._____

7. Industrial parks are usually located away from housing developments and downtown areas.   7._____

8. An advantage of working at home is that many costs are reduced or eliminated.   8._____

9. Your trade area is the area where all your competitors are located.   9._____

10. You can find possible locations for your business just by driving around your trade area.   10._____

Multiple Choice

Directions   In the Answers column, write the letter that represents the word, or group of words,
that correctly completes the statement.

Answers

1. Neighborhood shopping centers that house supermarkets, dry cleaners, and drugstores are
    (a) good locations for stores selling goods or services that people need to purchase
    frequently, (b) often called malls, (c) inconvenient for customers in the area, (d) not
    recommended for new business owners.   1._____

2. Anchor stores (a) are major tenants in shopping centers, (b) include department stores, large
    supermarkets, and large drugstores, (c) advertise heavily, (d) all of these.   2._____

3. All of the following describe super-regional shopping centers *except* (a) they house hundreds
    of stores, (b) they charge very high rents, (c) they are recommended for new business
    owners, (d) they service a large area.   3._____

4. Which of the following is *not* true about businesses operating in warehouses? (a) They are
    located near other retailers, (b) They have very low rent, (c) They do not have to look
    appealing on the inside, (d) They must advertise heavily.   4._____

5. In assessing a location, you should consider all of the following *except* (a) are other
    businesses thriving?(b) is it safe? (c) are there competitors?(d) is it attractive?   5._____

6. E-commerce consists of (a) doing business by e-mail, (b) buying and selling over the
    Internet, (c) offering customers electronic banking, (d) none of these.   6._____

7. A key factor in determining where an industrial business locates is (a) drive-by traffic,
    (b) availability of good employees, (c) adequate parking, (d) property of nearby businesses.   7._____

8. Industrial parks are usually located (a) where space is expensive, (b) near housing
    developments, (c) in downtown areas, (d) none of these.   8._____

9. Areas that suffer from lack of employment opportunities are (a) usually low-crime areas,
    (b) enterprise zones, (c) industrial parks, (d) always near community shopping centers.   9._____

10. Operating a home-based business (a) is cheaper than leasing business property, (b) increases
    networking opportunities, (c) makes business expansion easier, (d) all of these.   10._____

Problem Solving

Directions Answer the following questions in the space provided.

1. For each of the following businesses, decide what would be an appropriate location. Give reasons for your location selection.

   a. Florist

   _____

   _____

   _____

   _____

   b. Hardware store

   _____

   _____

   _____

   _____

   c. Hair salon

   _____

   _____

   _____

   _____

   d. Electronics manufacturer

   _____

   _____

   _____

   _____

   e. Office supply store

   _____

   _____

   _____

   _____

2. Why would a community want to attract industrial businesses by subsidizing rents?

   _____

   _____

   _____

   _____

Entrepreneurship: Ideas in Action, 5e, Student Edition

8.2 Obtain Space and Design the Physical Layout

True or False

Directions   Place a *T* for True or an *F* for False in the Answers column to show whether each
of the following statements is true or false.

Answers

1. Most entrepreneurs prefer to lease space for their businesses.   1. _____

2. For a gross lease, the landlord pays the property taxes and the tenant pays rent, insurance,   2. _____
   and any other expenses.

3. Rent per customer equals the amount of rent times the number of projected customers.   3. _____

4. In a percentage lease the tenant pays a base rent and a portion of their profits to the   4. _____
   landlord.

5. A scale drawing of your floor plan will help identify potential problems with your layout.   5. _____

6. Fluorescent lighting is the best choice of lighting for a bookstore.   6. _____

7. Visual merchandising combines products and atmosphere to encourage sales.   7. _____

8. Layout of an on-site service business is considered as carefully as that of a retail business. 8. _____

9. Wholesalers should design a layout that facilitates shipping and receiving.   9. _____

10. Attractiveness is the most important design factor for a manufacturing business.   10. _____

Multiple Choice

Directions   In the Answers column, write the letter that represents the word, or group of words,
that correctly completes the statement.

Answers

1. Most entrepreneurs lease business space because (a) it helps them obtain financing, (b) they   1. _____
   prefer to stay in a particular location, (c) they can't afford to purchase property, (d) all of these.

2. A lease in which the landlord pays all property expenses is a (a) net lease, (b) gross lease,   2. _____
   (c) tax-free lease, (d) percentage lease.

3. A lease in which the landlord receives a portion of the tenant's revenue each month in   3. _____
   addition to rent is a (a) net lease, (b) gross lease, (c) tax-free lease, (d) percentage lease.

4. A possible location for a business has rent of $975 per month and projected traffic of 9,600   4. _____
   customers per month. Rent per customer is (a) $0.08, (b) $0.10, (c) $0.98, (d) $0.11.

5. The layout, outside sign, and window displays of your business (a) should match your image,   5. _____
   (b) should be similar to other retail businesses in the area, (c) are less important than the
   name of your business, (d) should never be changed.

6. In designing a layout for a retail business, you should (a) not be concerned about areas   6. _____
   customers do not see, (b) place the cash register in the back of the store, (c) leave at least
   four feet of aisle space, (d) always use fluorescent lighting.

7. The goal of your layout should be to (a) attract customers to your store, (b) make their   7. _____
   shopping experience a pleasant one, (c) gain repeat business, (d) all of these.

8. The layout for an on-site service business (a) should emphasize organization, (b) is   8. _____
   unimportant, (c) should be similar to a retail business, (d) needs attractive window displays.

9. Wholesalers should (a) store merchandise by size, (b) store small items on the second floor,   9. _____
   (c) keep walkways free of merchandise, (d) not keep items too close to the shipping dock.

10. All of the following are important for a manufacturing business's layout *except*   10. _____
    (a) supervisors should sit near each other, (b) exits should be clearly marked, (c) hazardous
    materials should be stored safely, (d) work teams should be situated close together.

Problem Solving

Directions   Answer the following questions in the space provided.

1. Why do most businesses prefer to lease space rather than buy a building?

_____

_____

_____

_____

_____

2. Determine the rent per customer for each of the following.

Location	Rent per month	Projected customer traffic per month	Rent per customer
Downtown	$1,200	9,500	
Community shopping center	$2,800	18,000	
Stand-alone store	$1,050	7,400	

3. What would need to be included in a floor plan for a shop that sells and repairs bicycles and sells bicycle accessories?

_____

_____

_____

_____

_____

4. How can the layout of a wholesale business improve efficiency?

_____

_____

_____

_____

_____

5. Is a floor plan necessary for a home-based business? Why or why not?

_____

_____

_____

_____

_____

Name _____ Class _____ Date _____

8.3 Purchase Equipment, Supplies, and Inventory

True or False

Directions   Place a *T* for True or an *F* for False in the Answers column to show whether each of the following statements is true or false.

Answers

1. Inventory consists of the products and materials needed to make the product.   1. _____

2. A startup business should initially purchase the minimum quantity of equipment and supplies needed.   2. _____

3. Vendors are companies that sell products and services to businesses.   3. _____

4. Most suppliers have similar prices, so you need to get a quote from only one vendor.   4. _____

5. A quote is an estimate for how much you will pay for the good or service.   5. _____

6. All businesses must purchase inventory before they can open for business.   6. _____

7. For a manufacturing business, inventory includes merchandise purchased with the intent of either reselling it or using it to produce the company's product.   7. _____

8. A startup business should not tie up too much cash in inventory.   8. _____

9. Ongoing businesses usually have a good idea of how much inventory they need.   9. _____

10. A reorder point needs to be determined only for products that sell quickly.   10. _____

Multiple Choice

Directions   In the Answers column, write the letter that represents the word, or group of words, that correctly completes the statement.

Answers

1. Only some businesses need (a) office equipment, (b) office supplies, (c) furniture, (d) inventory.   1. _____

2. Sources of vendor information include all of the following *except* (a) the Internet, (b) insurance agencies, (c) trade magazines, (d) telephone directory.   2. _____

3. An estimate of how much you will pay for merchandise is (a) a quantity discount, (b) the financing terms, (c) a quote, (d) a letter of intent.   3. _____

4. Which of the following type of business does not always need inventory before it can open for business? (a) Service business, (b) Manufacturing business, (c) Retailing business, (d) Wholesaling business.   4. _____

5. For a retail business, inventory consists of (a) employee uniforms, (b) merchandise to be resold to customers, (c) parts needed to produce the business's product, (d) supplies.   5. _____

6. Determining the amount of inventory is particularly difficult for owners of new businesses because (a) their insurance may not cover damage to stored inventory, (b) they need to take advantage of quantity discounts, (c) they do not know what their level of sales will be, (d) all of these.   6. _____

7. To make sure you do not run out of stock unexpectedly, you can (a) establish a reorder point for each product you sell, (b) store extra inventory at a warehouse, (c) use only suppliers who guarantee to deliver in one day, (d) all of these.   7. _____

8. A reorder point is (a) an order to a supplier for additional items, (b) a predetermined level of inventory that signals when new stock must be purchased, (c) a reminder coded into a cash register, (d) none of these.   8. _____

Problem Solving

Directions   Answer the following questions in the space provided.

1. The first column of the following table lists the types of standard equipment and supply needs for most businesses. Complete the table by listing three items for each type of need.

Type	Items
Furniture	
Fixtures	
Office equipment	
Office supplies	
Maintenance supplies	
Kitchen supplies	

2. List five places where you can find information about vendors.

_____

_____

_____

_____

3. Describe the different types of inventory.

_____

_____

_____

_____

4. For each type of inventory, what are the consequences of being out of stock of a particular item?

_____

_____

_____

_____

5. How can a business manage its inventory so it does not run out of stock unexpectedly?

_____

_____

_____

_____

_____

Chapter 8 Assessment
Locate and Set Up Your Business

Vocabulary Review

Directions For each definition given, write the term defined in the appropriate squares.

1. A type of lease in which a tenant pays a percentage of revenue each month in addition to rent

   ☐☐☐☐☐☐☐☐☐☐☐☐☐   ☐☐☐☐☐☐

2. The area from which you expect to attract customers

   ☐☐☐☐☐☐☐   ☐☐☐☐☐

3. The merchandise a business sells to its customers

   ☐☐☐☐☐☐☐☐☐☐☐

4. A section of land that can be used for industrial business locations

   ☐☐☐☐☐☐☐☐☐☐☐☐   ☐☐☐☐☐

5. Person who owns and rents out buildings or space

   ☐☐☐☐☐☐☐☐☐☐

Fill-in-the-Blank

Directions For each item below, determine the word(s) that best complete the sentence. Write the word(s) in the Answers column.

Answers

1. Other businesses in a shopping center benefit from the advertising done by _____ stores.

   1._____

2. Because they do not need to look attractive on the inside, _____ are generally one of the least expensive rental facilities.

   2._____

3. The location of a(n) _____ business is as important as that of a retail business if customers visit the premises.

   3._____

4. A(n) _____ lease occurs when the landlord pays building insurance, and the tenant pays rent, taxes, and any other expenses.

   4._____

5. With a(n) _____ lease, the landlord covers all property expenses and the tenant pays only rent each month.

   5._____

6. You will need to prepare a(n) _____ drawing of the layout of your business.

   6._____

7. For all businesses, the location and layout need to be determined with the _____ in mind.

   7._____

8. To fill the standard and special equipment and supply needs of your business, you will have to research suppliers, or _____.

   8._____

9. Before you purchase merchandise for your business, you should get a(n) _____ or estimate of how much you will have to pay.

   9._____

10. The _____ point is a predetermined level of inventory when new stock must be purchased.

    10._____

Problem Solving

Directions   Lee Torres plans to open a retail pet store. The store will carry high-quality dog and cat foods; leashes, collars, and coats for dogs; scratching posts and trees for cats; carriers, beds, toys, treats, grooming needs, and flea products for both dogs and cats. Lee does not plan to sell puppies or kittens but will have a large assortment of birds, tropical fish, and small animals (hamsters, guinea pigs, and so on) and the foods and accessories needed for them. The store will also carry an assortment of books about the selection, training, and care of pets. Answer the following questions in the spaces provided.

1. If Lee's store will be in a large metropolitan area, what would be a good location for the business? Why?

    _____

    _____

    _____

    _____

2. If Lee's store will be in a small city or town, what would be a good location for the business? Why?

    _____

    _____

    _____

    _____

    _____

3. What are some general considerations for the layout of the pet store?

    _____

    _____

    _____

    _____

4. In the box below, design a layout of the store. *Student layouts will vary.*

Entrepreneurship: Ideas in Action, 5e, Student Edition

9.1 Finance Your Business

True or False

Directions   Place a *T* for True or an *F* for False in the Answers column to show whether each of the following statements is true or false.

Answers

1. Money loaned to a business with the understanding that the money will be repaid is called equity capital.

1. _____

2. Debt capital is money invested in a business in return for a share of the business's profits.

2. _____

3. Net worth is the difference between what you owe and what you own.

3. _____

4. Venture capitalists are usually interested in companies that have the potential of earning hundreds of millions of dollars within a few years.

4. _____

5. Your company's debt-to-equity ratio measures how much money you can safely borrow.

5. _____

6. Banks require collateral for most unsecured loans.

6. _____

7. Equity capital is money invested in a business without expectation of a share of the profits.

7. _____

8. A solid business plan is needed for a bank loan but not for SBA loan assistance.

8. _____

9. Most SBA loan assistance is made by guaranteeing loans made by commercial banks.

9. _____

10. Entrepreneurs may be able to get financial assistance from their state or local governments.

10. _____

Multiple Choice

Directions   In the Answers column, write the letter that represents the word, or group of words, that correctly completes the statement.

Answers

1. To calculate net worth, you should (a) prepare a personal financial statement, (b) prepare a pro forma financial statement, (c) calculate debt-to-equity ratio, (d) none of these.

1. _____

2. Things that you own are called (a) liabilities, (b) net worth, (c) equity, (d) assets.

2. _____

3. Money invested in a business in return for a share of the business's profits is (a) investment capital, (b) equity capital, (c) venture capital, (d) debt capital.

3. _____

4. Venture capitalists are individuals or companies that (a) make a living investing in startup companies, (b) have few requirements for lending money, (c) are sponsored by the SBA, (d) help small businesses find investors.

4. _____

5. Unsecured loans are (a) backed by collateral, (b) usually interest free, (c) usually paid back within a short period of time, (d) easier to get than secured loans.

5. _____

6. A line of credit (a) is a type of secured loan, (b) has a fee whether or not money is borrowed, (c) is a type of debt capital, (d) all of these.

6. _____

7. If a business wants to make improvements to increase profits, it will usually get a (a) line of credit, (b) long-term loan, (c) startup loan, (d) short-term loan.

7. _____

8. A bank may turn down a loan application for a new business because the entrepreneur (a) is too confident, (b) has previously owned a business, (c) is investing too little personal money in the business, (d) none of these.

8. _____

9. MESBICs lend money to small businesses that are (a) in redevelopment areas, (b) in manufacturing industries, (c) owned by members of ethnic minorities, (d) in rural areas.

9. _____

10. Although similar to borrowing from the SBA, the restrictions are tighter for borrowing from (a) HUD, (b) state governments, (c) the EDA, (d) local governments.

10. _____

Problem Solving

Directions Answer the following questions in the space provided.

1. Explain the difference between debt capital and equity capital.

_____

_____

_____

_____

_____

2. List five sources of debt capital.

_____

_____

_____

_____

_____

3. List four sources of equity capital.

_____

_____

_____

_____

_____

4. Do you think it is better for an entrepreneur to finance a business with debt capital or equity capital? Explain your answer.

_____

_____

_____

_____

_____

5. Describe a secured loan and an unsecured loan and list four kinds of secured loans.

_____

_____

_____

_____

_____

9.2 Pro Forma Financial Statements

True or False

Directions   Place a *T* for True or an *F* for False in the Answers column to show whether each of the following statements is true or false.

Answers

1. A cash flow statement describes a business's revenue and expenses over a period of time.   1._____

2. A best-case-scenario cash flow statement should project the lowest revenues and highest expenses that your business is likely to have.   2._____

3. An income statement shows revenues you have received and expenses you have paid.   3._____

4. The cost of the inventory a business sells during a particular period is called cost of goods sold.   4._____

5. Pro forma income statements help lenders see the long-term growth of your business.   5._____

6. Loans and accounts payable are examples of liabilities.   6._____

7. Inventory is a type of fixed asset because it will be used up in normal business operations.   7._____

8. A utility bill is a type of current liability known as an account payable.   8._____

9. A business that has more assets than liabilities has negative net worth.   9._____

10. Illiquid assets are easily converted into cash.   10._____

Multiple Choice

Directions   In the Answers column, write the letter that represents the word, or group of words, that correctly completes the statement.

Answers

1. Expenses that are incurred by a business every month are (a) startup costs, (b) operating expenses, (c) short-term expenses, (d) accounts payable.   1._____

2. During the first few months of operating a new business, the cash flow is usually (a) positive, (b) unknown, (c) estimated, (d) negative.   2._____

3. The difference between revenue and cost of goods sold is called (a) gross profit, (b) owner's equity, (c) cost of goods sold, (d) accounts receivable.   3._____

4. An income statement indicates (a) actual cash coming in and going out, (b) how much money a business earns or loses during a particular period, (c) expenses you have not yet received, (d) your total current assets.   4._____

5. The assets, liabilities, and capital of a business are shown on a(n) (a) income statement, (b) profit and loss statement, (c) balance sheet, (d) cash flow statement.   5._____

6. In the accounting equation, assets must always equal (a) liabilities plus owner's equity, (b) liabilities minus owner's equity, (c) owner's equity minus liabilities, (d) current liabilities plus long-term liabilities.   6._____

7. On a balance sheet, buildings and furniture would be included as (a) long-term liabilities, (b) fixed assets, (c) current assets, (d) accounts receivable.   7._____

8. A mortgage is a type of (a) current liability, (b) account payable, (c) long-term liability, (d) fixed asset.   8._____

9. Depreciation is included on a balance sheet to show that (a) some accounts are uncollectible, (b) some assets have been sold, (c) some fixed assets have lost value over time, (d) some expenses have not been paid.   9._____

10. A business owner's private net worth is shown on (a) an income statement, (b) a balance statement, (c) a personal financial statement, (d) none of these.   10._____

Problem Solving

Directions Answer the following questions in the space provided.

1. The following table lists items that appear on various financial statements. Complete the table by identifying the financial statement on which the item should appear.

Item	Financial Statement
Utility expenses due	
Cash received for goods sold	
Accounts payable	
Depreciation	
Rent paid	
Forecasted revenues	
Uncollectible accounts	
Insurance paid	

2. Many of the items included on a list of startup costs also appear on a balance sheet. Why?

_____

_____

_____

_____

_____

_____

3. Explain the difference between accounts receivable and accounts payable.

_____

_____

_____

_____

_____

_____

4. Write the accounting equation and define each element in it.

_____

_____

_____

_____

_____

_____

9.3 Recordkeeping for Businesses

True or False

Directions Place a *T* for True or an *F* for False in the Answers column to show whether each of the following statements is true or false.

Answers

1. Under the cash method of accounting, revenue is recorded prior to receipt. 1._____

2. The accrual method of accounting requires you to record only those transactions that are paid. 2._____

3. Journals are accounting records of the transactions that you make. 3._____

4. Subsidiary ledgers are commonly used for accounts receivable and accounts payable. 4._____

5. An aging table is a recordkeeping tool for tracking accounts receivable. 5._____

6. You should balance your check register every three months when you receive your statement from the bank. 6._____

7. Any checks or deposits that are not listed on your bank statement are classified as reconciled. 7._____

8. Payroll records show employee earnings and any deductions from those earnings. 8._____

9. Deductions from employee's earnings include federal, state, and local taxes and contributions for social security and Medicare. 9._____

10. A business that collects sales tax must pay the tax quarterly. 10._____

Multiple Choice

Directions In the Answers column, write the letter that represents the word, or group of words, that correctly completes the statement.

Answers

1. A sales journal is used to record only (a) purchases of merchandise on account, (b) sales of merchandise on account, (c) cash payment transactions, (d) cash receipt transactions. 1._____

2. The journal used to record any type of transaction is the (a) sales journal, (b) cash payments journal, (c) general journal, (d) ledger journal. 2._____

3. Copying information from a journal entry to a ledger account is (a) posting, (b) done on the first of each month, (c) summarizing accounts, (d) financing. 3._____

4. An accounting record that summarizes all the information for a particular business item is (a) a subsidiary ledger, (b) a journal, (c) an account, (d) a general ledger. 4._____

5. If you have a personal checking account, you (a) can use the same account for your business, (b) should still get a separate business account, (c) should get a separate check register for business transactions, (d) will not get a separate bank statement for a business account. 5._____

6. A booklet in which you record the dates and amounts of the checks you have written is called a(n) (a) aging account, (b) subsidiary ledger, (c) check register, (d) payroll register. 6._____

7. A payroll register includes all of the following information except (a) an employee's regular and overtime earnings, (b) federal taxes deducted from an employee's earnings, (c) sales taxes deducted from an employee's earnings, (d) an employee's social security contribution. 7._____

8. A business must pay income taxes (a) at the end of each month, (b) even when it does not earn a profit, (c) twice a year, (d) quarterly. 8._____

Problem Solving

Directions   Answer the following questions in the space provided.

1. Name and describe the five different journals that businesses use to record their transactions.

_____

_____

_____

_____

_____

_____

_____

_____

_____

_____

_____

_____

_____

_____

_____

2. For each of the following business activities, identify all the places where the activity should be recorded.

Business Activity	Journal	Ledger	Other
Purchase of merchandise on account			
Payment of utility bill			
Cash sale			
Weekly deposit of cash and checks			
Sale of merchandise on account			
Payment of employee wages			

Entrepreneurship: Ideas in Action, 5e, Student Edition

Chapter 9 Assessment
Plan and Track Your Finances

Vocabulary Review

Directions   In each of the following sentences, the underlined term is not used correctly. In the space provided, rewrite the sentence so the term is used correctly.

1. Liabilities are items of value that are owned by a business, such as cash, equipment, and inventory.

2. To provide an accurate statement of the value of liabilities on a balance sheet, a company should include an allowance for depreciation.

3. For an unsecured loan, a bank requires collateral, such as real estate or an insurance policy.

Fill-in-the-Blank

Directions   For each item below, determine the word(s) that best complete the sentence. Write the word(s) in the Answers column.

Answers

1. Financial statements based on projections are known as _____ financial statements.

   1._____

2. _____ expenses are incurred by a business every month, such as salaries and rent.

   2._____

3. The assets, liabilities, and capital of a business at a particular point in time are shown on a(n) _____.

   3._____

4. Payments due for products or services purchased on credit by customers are _____.

   4._____

5. A(n) _____ loan is made for a very specific purpose and is repaid within a year.

   5._____

6. Banks often reject loan applicants who do not have a solid _____.

   6._____

7. The dollar value of the goods or services a business sells to customers is called _____.

   7._____

8. Inventory is a kind of asset that can be converted into _____.

   8._____

9. A(n) _____ is any business activity that changes assets, liabilities, or net worth.

   9._____

10. A(n) _____ is a list of people who receive salary or wage payments from a business.

   10._____

Problem Solving

Directions   Answer the following questions in the space provided.

1. Name and describe the kinds of tax records a business must keep.

_____

_____

_____

_____

_____

_____

_____

_____

_____

2. A startup business estimates first-year revenues at $93,000. The following amounts are estimates of operating expenses for that year: cost of goods sold, $41,200; rent, $11,400; utilities, $1,080; salaries, $18,000; advertising, $950; supplies, $500; insurance, $1,800; other, $350.

   a. What are the total estimated operating expenses? Show your work in the space provided.

   b. What amount of income should be shown on the pro forma income statement? Show your work in the space provided.

3. A retail pet store has $10,500 in cash and inventory worth $31,250. The store has a six-year bank loan of $40,000 and current liabilities of $360. The office equipment for the store is worth $10,500, less $1,150 in depreciation; store fixtures are worth $8,700, less $600 in depreciation; and a company vehicle is worth $10,500, less $1,500 in depreciation. Accounts receivable are $1,050 and accounts payable are $9,800.

   a. What are the store's current assets, fixed assets, and total assets? Show your work in the space provided.

   b. What are the store's current liabilities, long-term liabilities, and total liabilities? Show your work in the space provided.

   c. What is the owner's equity? Show your work in the space provided.

10.1 Operating Procedures

True or False

Directions   Place a *T* for True or an *F* for False in the Answers column to show whether each of the following statements is true or false.

Answers

1. Management is the process of achieving goals by doing all the work yourself.

   1._____

2. Strategic planning is most important in the short-term.

   2._____

3. Organizational structure is a plan that shows how the various jobs in a company relate to one another.

   3._____

4. The authoritative management style is often used in a crisis situation when there is not enough time to let the group participate in the decision-making process.

   4._____

5. Good managers understand that all employees prefer to be involved in day-to-day decision making.

   5._____

6. As part of the control function, you will routinely review your plans and make adjustments.

   6._____

7. A detailed operations manual is an essential tool for operating your business effectively.

   7._____

8. Rules are more specific than procedures.

   8._____

9. Democratic management style includes procedures in which employees are invited to vote on company rules and regulations.

   9._____

10. Instruction in safety procedures should be part of employee training.

    10._____

Multiple Choice

Directions   In the Answers column, write the letter that represents the word, or group of words, that correctly completes the statement.

Answers

1. Rules, policies, and procedures, are important components of (a) long-term planning, (b) intermediate-term planning, (c) short-term planning, (d) none of these.

   1._____

2. All of the following are included in the organizing function *except* (a) assigning tasks, (b) hiring employees, (c) grouping tasks into departments, (d) allocating resources.

   2._____

3. Training and compensating the employees of a business is part of which management function? (a) Staffing, (b) Planning, (c) Implementing, (d) Controlling.

   3._____

4. The management style *most* appropriate to use with a new group of employees who do not have previous experience in the type of work being performed is (a) mixed management, (b) participatory management, (c) democratic management, (d) authoritative management.

   4._____

5. If standards are not being met, a manager may need to (a) hire new employees, (b) upgrade to higher-quality production materials, (c) change operating procedures, (d) all of these.

   5._____

6. "Employees may smoke only in designated smoking areas" is an example of a company (a) rule, (b) procedure, (c) directive, (d) policy.

   6._____

7. Business rules, policies, and procedures should be included (a) in your business plan, (b) on the home page of your company's Web site, (c) in your operations manual, (d) all of these.

   7._____

8. A policy for replacements, refunds, or repairs (a) is usually not necessary for most businesses, (b) will help maintain customer goodwill, (c) negatively impacts profits, (d) should never be made public.

   8._____

Problem Solving

Directions Answer the following questions in the space provided.

1. Name and describe the five functions of management.

    _____

    _____

    _____

    _____

    _____

    _____

    _____

    _____

    _____

    _____

2. The table below lists five tasks often performed by managers. Name which one of the five functions of management is represented by each task.

Task	Management Function
Deciding which job you will assign to which employee	
Hiring a new employee	
Completing the monthly budget	
Conducting a yearly performance appraisal for an employee	
Writing a memo to an employee instructing her how to accomplish a task	

3. Zhang Wei operates a Chinese restaurant and is thinking about offering delivery services for carry out orders. What kinds of things must he plan before offering a delivery service?

    _____

    _____

    _____

    _____

    _____

    _____

    _____

    _____

Entrepreneurship: Ideas in Action, 5e, Student Edition

10.2 Inventory Management

True or False

Directions Place a *T* for True or an *F* for False in the Answers column to show whether each of the following statements is true or false.

Answers

1. The most important aspect of inventory management is having items in stock when needed. 1._____

2. A business should track its inventory using either the perpetual inventory method or the physical inventory method but not both. 2._____

3. An inventory record for an item can be kept on a stock card or in an electronic format. 3._____

4. Businesses that sell more than 50 different items usually use a computer to track inventory. 4._____

5. Taking a physical inventory means counting the number of items you have in stock. 5._____

6. The amount of inventory recorded when taking a physical inventory will always be the same as the amount recorded in a perpetual inventory system. 6._____

7. If a business uses a periodic inventory method, it does not need to take a physical inventory. 7._____

8. Point-of-sale software updates inventory as each sale is made. 8._____

9. Businesses must weigh the cost of being out of stock with the cost of carrying more inventory. 9._____

10. The stock turnover rate shows how many times a year a business sells all of its merchandise. 10._____

Multiple Choice

Directions In the Answers column, write the letter that represents the word, or group of words, that correctly completes the statement.

Answers

1. The amount of inventory you need to purchase can be calculated from the (a) sales forecast, (b) balance sheet, (c) cash flow statement, (d) income statement. 1._____

2. All of the following should be recorded on an inventory record *except* (a) item's cost, (b) the item's stock number, (c) current amount of inventory, (d) maximum inventory amount. 2._____

3. The reorder point of an item is (a) the current amount of inventory, (b) the maximum inventory amount, (c) the minimum inventory amount, (d) the date inventory was ordered. 3._____

4. If inventory is held too long it may become (a) out of stock, (b) deteriorated, (c) obsolete, (d) an insurance risk. 4._____

5. A low stock report shows (a) that a physical inventory should be taken, (b) the number of units of each item to order, (c) the number of units sold, (d) when items should be ordered. 5._____

6. The level of inventory you keep in stock depends on (a) the frequency with which you sell your inventory, (b) the cost of carrying inventory, (c) the cost of losing a sale because you are out of stock, (d) all of these. 6._____

7. The costs of holding inventory are (a) deteriorating costs, (b) fixed costs, (c) carrying costs, (d) stock turnover costs. 7._____

8. If an item is out of stock, you may (a) increase carrying costs, (b) lose customer loyalty, (c) have higher insurance costs, (d) have to change your inventory method. 8._____

9. The stock turnover rate (a) shows how many times a year you sell all of your merchandise, (b) is the same for every industry, (c) should be calculated monthly, (d) all of these. 9._____

10. If the stock turnover rate for your industry is 3, you should keep ___ months worth of inventory in stock at all times. (a) 2, (b) 3, (c) 4, (d) 9. 10._____

Problem Solving

Directions   Answer the following questions in the space provided.

1. How does the type of business help to determine the method used for tracking inventory?

_____

_____

_____

_____

_____

_____

_____

2. How does the product or service of a business help to determine the method used for tracking inventory?

_____

_____

_____

_____

_____

_____

3. What other factors might influence a business's choice of inventory tracking method?

_____

_____

_____

_____

_____

_____

4. Explain how carrying costs, out-of-stock costs, and the stock turnover rate each contributes to determining the level of inventory a business should keep in stock.

_____

_____

_____

_____

_____

_____

10.3 Financial Management

True or False

Directions   Place a *T* for True or an *F* for False in the Answers column to show whether each of the following statements is true or false.

Answers

1. A cash budget is based on past revenues and will show the projection of incoming cash.   1._____

2. If your cash receipts will not cover your expenses, you can try to increase the cash coming into your business.   2._____

3. To encourage customers to pay more quickly, you can offer discounts on bills paid immediately.   3._____

4. Reducing your payroll expenses by laying off workers can improve your cash flow.   4._____

5. You can reduce fixed expenses to improve your cash flow.   5._____

6. Dividing total sales by the sales of a specific product gives the percent of sales accounted for by that product.   6._____

7. Net profit on sales is found by dividing net income after taxes by net sales.   7._____

8. Net sales is the dollar amount of all sales, including sales that have been returned.   8._____

9. The profit ratio for a business can be compared to the average profit ratio for the industry.   9._____

10. Below the breakeven point, revenues are greater than expenses, and you will lose money.   10._____

Multiple Choice

Directions   In the Answers column, write the letter that represents the word, or group of words, that correctly completes the statement.

Answers

1. Offering discounts on bills paid right away will (a) increase your cash receipts, (b) get customers to pay more quickly, (c) reduce your accounts receivable, (d) all of these.   1._____

2. You can reduce your disbursements by (a) holding more inventory, (b) adding to your payroll, (c) paying your bills more promptly, (d) none of these.   2._____

3. Reducing your inventory will (a) decrease your accounts payable, (b) increase your accounts payable, (c) decrease your accounts receivable, (d) not improve your cash flow.   3._____

4. Analyzing your sales by product can help you (a) determine the amount of income tax to pay, (b) find the breakeven point, (c) make decisions about what kind of inventory to stock, (d) determine whether or not your business is earning a profit.   4._____

5. All of the information necessary for calculating net profit on sales is found on the (a) cash flow statement, (b) balance sheet, (c) income statement, (d) inventory record.   5._____

6. What must be subtracted from net sales to find gross profit? (a) Cost of goods sold, (b) Operating expenses, (c) Total expenses, (d) Interest expense.   6._____

7. Net profit on sales is equal to net income after taxes divided by (a) gross sales, (b) cost of goods sold, (c) net sales, (d) none of these.   7._____

8. The volume of sales that must be made to cover all the expenses of a business is (a) the breakeven point, (b) impossible to determine, (c) net revenue from sales, (d) the profit point.   8._____

9. You can increase cash receipts by (a) establishing tighter credit policies, (b) following up on unpaid accounts receivable, (c) holding shipments to customers with unpaid bills, (d) all of these.   9._____

10. The net-profit-on-sales ratio determines (a) cash flow, (b) the breakeven point, (c) business profits, (d) interest expense.   10._____

Problem Solving

Directions Answer the following questions in the space provided.

1. Complete the following income statement.

Revenue from sales	
Gross sales	$183,000
Returns	$1,900
Net sales	
Cost of goods sold	$74,400
Gross profit	
Operating expenses	
Salaries	$32,400
Advertising	$1,200
Rent	$12,000
Utilities	$900
Insurance	$1,200
Other	$780
Total expenses	
Net income from operations	
Interest expense	$3,600
Net income before taxes	
Taxes	$13,350
Net income after taxes	

2. Use the income statement from Question 1 to compute net profit on sales. Show your work in the space below.

3. A pet store owner analyzes sales by department in order to determine whether inventory should be increased or reduced. Determine the total sales, find the percent of sales for each department, and record your answers in the table that follows.

Department	Sales	Percent of Total Sales
Birds	$45,900	
Small animals	$25,800	
Tropical fish	$39,800	
Cats	$81,200	
Dogs	$78,300	
Total		

Entrepreneurship: Ideas in Action, 5e, Student Edition

Chapter 10 Assessment
Operations Management

Vocabulary Review

Directions In each of the following sentences, the underlined term is not used correctly. Rewrite the sentence so the term is used correctly.

1. An <u>organizational structure</u> is a plan that shows the salaries of all company employees.

2. Net income after taxes is found by subtracting cost of goods sold from <u>gross profit</u>.

3. The <u>periodic inventory method</u> keeps track of inventory levels on a daily basis.

Fill-in-the-Blank

Directions For each item below, determine the word(s) that best complete the sentence. Write the word(s) in the Answers column.

Answers

1. A cash budget should be based on _____ past revenue and operating expenses.

   1. _____

2. A business can use a(n) _____ to track down customers who owe money to the business.

   2. _____

3. If your business has cash flow problems, you should check to make sure that you are not holding too much _____.

   3. _____

4. Setting broad, long-range objectives to achieve the long-term goals of your business is called _____ planning.

   4. _____

5. A(n) _____ statement shows whether or not a business is earning a profit and the amount of the profit or loss.

   5. _____

6. To calculate your net profit on sales, you need to know your net income after taxes and your _____.

   6. _____

7. At the breakeven point, your sales are _____ your expenses.

   7. _____

8. _____ is the process of achieving goals by establishing operating procedures that make effective use of people and other resources.

   8. _____

9. The process of setting standards for the operation of a business and ensuring those standards are met is called _____.

   9. _____

10. _____ outline the appropriate behavior and actions of those who work for you.

    10. _____

Problem Solving

Directions Answer the following questions in the space provided.

1. You own and manage a small retail toy store. You have two employees, who have worked with you for more than 10 years. Because business has been good, you have recently added two new employees, neither of whom has any prior sales experience. What management style will you use with your staff? Explain.

_____

_____

_____

_____

2. Complete the following cash budget.

	A	B	C	D
		Estimated	**Actual**	**Difference**
1	**Cash receipts**			
2	Cash sales	$4,600	$5,900	
3	Accounts receivable payments	$8,280	$9,350	
4	**Total cash receipts**			
5	**Cash disbursements**			
6	Salaries	$3,500	$6,200	
7	Gasoline	$2,700	$3,100	
8	Rent	$1,000	$1,000	
9	Utilities	$75	$83	
10	Advertising	$200	$175	
11	Supplies	$40	$64	
12	Insurance	$100	$100	
13	Other	$65	$82	
14	**Total cash disbursements**			
15	**Net cash increase/decrease**			

3. What does the cash budget show about the company's cash flow? How can the cash flow be improved?

_____

_____

_____

_____

Entrepreneurship: Ideas in Action, 5e, Student Edition

11.1 Identify Your Staffing Needs

True or False

Directions Place a *T* for True or an *F* for False in the Answers column to show whether each
of the following statements is true or false.

Answers

1. The people who work for your business are your human resources. 1._____

2. Implementing involves determining the number of employees you need and defining
   a process for hiring them. 2._____

3. A collection of tasks is called a job. 3._____

4. A job description is the process of determining the tasks and sequence of tasks necessary to
   perform a job. 4._____

5. An organizational structure shows how various jobs in a company related to each other. 5._____

6. The owner of a large company with many employees should not have to deal with
   relatively unimportant issues. 6._____

7. The best way for an entrepreneur to recruit employees is through college placement centers. 7._____

8. Employment agencies typically charge businesses and/or the job seekers a fee when they
   are successful in making a match. 8._____

9. Online recruiting is generally the least expensive way to find employees for your business. 9._____

10. Hiring employees is usually not too difficult because you have enough information to make
    an effective decision. 10._____

Multiple Choice

Directions In the Answers column, write the letter that represents the word, or group of words,
that correctly completes the statement.

Answers

1. To determine your staffing needs, (a) create an organizational chart, (b) make a list of all the
   duties in your business and the time needed to perform each, (c) write a detailed job
   description for each job, (d) determine how much money to offer applicants. 1._____

2. An employment specialist who seeks out highly qualified professionals to fill positions is
   called a (a) human resources manager, (b) entrepreneur, (c) headhunter, (d) job counselor. 2._____

3. An organizational chart can help the owner of a company (a) analyze staffing needs,
   (b) recruit employees, (c) obtain referrals, (d) none of these. 3._____

4. Who reports to whom in a company is called the (a) line of succession, (b) chain of
   command, (c) career pathway, (d) ladder of success. 4._____

5. Looking for people to hire and attracting them to the business is called (a) controlling,
   (b) implementing, (c) employing, (d) recruiting. 5._____

6. A want ad should do all of the following *except* (a) briefly describe the position, (b) ask
   applicants to identify their race and religion, (c) identify any special job requirements,
   (d) request resumes from applicants. 6._____

7. One of the best ways entrepreneurs can find employees is through (a) employment agencies,
   (b) want ads, (c) referrals from friends or employees, (d) college placement centers. 7._____

8. Students who work for little or no pay in order to gain experience are (a) freelancers,
   (b) interns, (c) trainees, (d) available through employment agencies. 8._____

Problem Solving

Directions   Answer the following questions in the space provided.

1. In the table below, identify six resources that an employer can use to recruit employees. For each, list one advantage and one disadvantage.

Resource	Advantage	Disadvantage

2. Distinguish between a job, a task, and a function.

_____

_____

_____

_____

_____

_____

_____

_____

3. Describe some advantages of working as a freelance employee. What are some possible disadvantages?

_____

_____

_____

_____

_____

_____

_____

_____

_____

_____

_____

Entrepreneurship: Ideas in Action, 5e, Student Edition

11.2 Staff Your Business

True or False

Directions   Place a *T* for True or an *F* for False in the Answers column to show whether each of the following statements is true or false.

Answers

1. During the interview, it's not helpful to "sell your business" to the prospective employee.   1._____

2. It is important to make the most of the job interview because you want to hire employees who can improve your ability to meet customer needs.   2._____

3. Warning signs that a person may not be a good worker include frequent job changes, unexplained gaps in employment, and critical comments about previous employers.   3._____

4. In the job interview, it is okay to make a snap judgment when you know immediately that the candidate is not right for the job.   4._____

5. When checking references, you should ask previous employers about a candidate's personal qualities.   5._____

6. Wages, which are fixed amounts of pay per hour or per unit, are paid on a weekly basis, and salaries, which are fixed amounts of pay for a year, are paid on a monthly basis.   6._____

7. An employee can receive a bonus regardless of whether he or she is paid a wage or a salary.   7._____

8. A commission combination plan includes a base salary plus commission.   8._____

9. Employees often abuse paid sick leave, so businesses only offer five paid sick days a year.   9._____

10. The OSH Act requires employers to maintain safe working conditions for their employees.   10._____

Multiple Choice

Directions   In the Answers column, write the letter that represents the word, or group of words, that correctly completes the statement.

Answers

1. Rewards, other than cash are called (a) bonuses, (b) raises, (c) benefits, (d) commissions.   1._____

2. During a job interview, you should (a) check references, (b) use the job description to prepare questions, (c) allow the applicant plenty of time to talk, (d) offer the job if you are impressed with the applicant.   2._____

3. In making a job offer, you should clearly state the (a) benefits, (b) terms of employment, (c) starting salary, (d) all of these.   3._____

4. A compensation package should include (a) vacation time, (b) terms of employment, (c) wages or salary, (d) all of these.   4._____

5. In most markets, wages and salaries are determined (a) by large companies, (b) biweekly, (c) by the government, (d) competitively.   5._____

6. An organization that represent employees and bargains on their behalf for better working conditions is called a (a) collective bargaining unit, (b) union, (c) mediation group, (d) workers' right's group.   6._____

7. The Family and Medical Leave Act of 1993 grants up to three months unpaid leave if an employee has (a) given birth, (b) a serious health condition, (c) adopted a child, (d) all of these.   7._____

8. The Fair Labor Standards Act (a) establishes the maximum number of hours employees can work, (b) promotes employment of older persons, (c) prohibits hiring discrimination on the basis of race, (d) requires employers to verify that employees are American citizens.   8._____

Problem Solving

Directions   Answer the following questions in the space provided.

1. What is the difference between wages and salaries?

    _____

    _____

    _____

    _____

    _____

    _____

2. Describe the advantages to the employee and to the employer for each type of pay listed in the following table.

Type of Pay	Advantages for Employee	Advantages for Employer
Wage		
Salary		
Commission-only salary		
Base salary or wage plus commission		
Bonus		

3. Describe the types of benefits offered by businesses. Which are usually offered only by large companies?

    _____

    _____

    _____

    _____

    _____

    _____

    _____

    _____

    _____

Entrepreneurship: Ideas in Action, 5e, Student Edition

11.3 Direct and Control Human Resources

True or False

Directions Place a *T* for True or an *F* for False in the Answers column to show whether each of the following statements is true or false.

Answers

1. Effective managers need good leadership qualities.   1._____

2. Supervisory-level managers have the highest level of responsibility in a company.   2._____

3. Theory Y managers use the democratic management style.   3._____

4. An employee who does not follow established policies concerning vacations, holidays, hours, and acceptable dress should be dismissed immediately.   4._____

5. All new employees should go through a training program as soon as they are hired, but qualified employees should not need any additional training.   5._____

6. Coaching is a training technique in which one employee teams up with another, more experienced employee to learn a job.   6._____

7. One way to motivate employees is to give them adequate responsibility.   7._____

8. If a company is to expand, the owner must delegate workloads and responsibilities.   8._____

9. A performance evaluation is part of the implementing function of management.   9._____

10. Managers should not take the opinions and feedback of their employees into consideration when making important decisions.   10._____

Multiple Choice

Directions In the Answers column, write the letter that represents the word, or group of words, that correctly completes the statement.

Answers

1. Which managers work directly with the workers on the job? (a) Supervisory-level managers, (b) Middle managers, (c) Top-level managers, (d) All of these.   1._____

2. Theory Z managers (a) use the democratic management style, (b) don't like to delegate, (c) place more emphasis on group decision-making, (d) empower workers with pep talks.   2._____

3. Employee training should (a) begin as soon as the employee is hired, (b) be evaluated to ensure it was effective, (c) be continuous, (d) all of these.   3._____

4. Employees learn new techniques and trends from an expert in the field (a) during on-the-job training, (b) in coaching sessions, (c) at conferences and seminars, (d) called a mentor.   4._____

5. With this training technique, employees receive feedback and instruction from their manager on a constant basis. (a) On-the-job training, (b) Coaching, (c) Mentoring, (d) Shadowing.   5._____

6. All of the following are ways to motivate your employees *except* (a) pay them well, (b) give them less responsibility, (c) treat them fairly, (d) provide public recognition for good work.   6._____

7. It is important to listen to your employees because (a) they may be able to offer fresh ideas, (b) they can help you delegate responsibility, (c) they may not want to follow new procedures, (d) you will be able to create a better evaluation procedure.   7._____

8. You should evaluate employee performance (a) once a month, (b) on a job analysis form, (c) to help you identify both outstanding and problem employees, (d) none of these.   8._____

9. Promotion decisions should be (a) made fairly, (b) based on employee competition, (c) made at a team meeting, (d) made using the formal decision-making process.   9._____

10. Once you decide to dismiss an employee, you should (a) issue a written warning, (b) tell the employee immediately, (c) tell the employee publicly, (d) explain your decision to other employees.   10._____

Problem Solving

Directions Answer the following questions in the space provided.

1. Why might the owner of a manufacturing company establish a company policy requiring all employees to wear protective eye and ear gear?

     _____

     _____

     _____

     _____

2. Why might the owner of a nursery and garden supply center not allow employees to take vacations between April and October?

     _____

     _____

     _____

     _____

3. How does a business owner benefit from delegating authority?

     _____

     _____

     _____

     _____

4. How does a business owner benefit from listening to employees?

     _____

     _____

     _____

     _____

5   How does an employer benefit from a yearly evaluation of an employee?

     _____

     _____

     _____

     _____

6. How does an employee benefit from a yearly evaluation by an employer?

     _____

     _____

     _____

     _____

Chapter 11 Assessment
Human Resource Management

Vocabulary Review

Directions For each definition given, write the term defined in the appropriate squares.

1. Payments for labor or services that are made on an hourly, daily, or per-unit basis

   ☐☐☐☐☐

2. To look for people to hire

   ☐☐☐☐☐☐

3. Payments for labor or services done on an annual basis

   ☐☐☐☐☐☐☐☐

4. Written statement listing the duties and responsibilities of a job

   ☐☐☐☐ ☐☐☐☐☐☐☐☐☐☐☐

5. Managers who trust and respect their employees and value their contributions

   ☐☐☐☐☐☐ ☐ ☐☐☐☐☐☐☐☐☐

Fill-in-the-Blank

Directions For each item below, determine the word(s) that best complete the sentence. Write the word(s) in the Answers column.

Answers

1. A(n) _____ structure is a plan that shows how the various jobs in a company relate to one another.

   1. _____

2. One of the best ways to find employees is to act on _____ from friends, acquaintances, or employees.

   2. _____

3. You should review the job candidate's _____ just before the interview begins.

   3. _____

4. Profit _____ is a compensation arrangement in which employees are paid a portion of the company's profits.

   4. _____

5. A financial reward in addition to a regular wage or salary is a(n) _____.

   5. _____

6. A(n) _____ is a percentage of a sale paid to a salesperson.

   6. _____

7. A classified advertisement an employer places in the newspaper to attract job applicants is called a(n) _____.

   7. _____

8. In _____, one employee teams up with another, more experienced employee to learn a job.

   8. _____

9. _____ managers serve as a liaison between supervisory-level and top-level managers.

   9. _____

10. Performance reviews should be recorded on _____ forms.

    10. _____

Problem Solving

Directions   Answer the following questions in the spaces provided.

1.   Which two steps in the hiring process do you think are most important? Give reasons for your answers.

_____

_____

_____

_____

_____

_____

2.   Which leadership quality do you think is most important? Why?

_____

_____

_____

_____

_____

_____

3.   Which way of motivating employees do you think is most effective? Why?

_____

_____

_____

_____

_____

_____

4.   How can an employer use the yearly performance evaluation as motivation?

_____

_____

_____

_____

_____

_____

12.1 Business Risks

True or False

Directions   Place a *T* for True or an *F* for False in the Answers column to show whether each of the following statements is true or false.

Answers

1. If you practice risk management you are assuring your business will never face a loss.
   1._____

2. You should let your managers and employees know about your plan for handling risks.
   2._____

3. Theft is one of the risks that business owners face, and it is impossible to protect yourself against the different kinds of theft.
   3._____

4. Risk assessment involves looking at all aspects of a business and determining possible risks.
   4._____

5. Electronic devices and security guards are the only steps you can take to prevent or reduce shoplifting.
   5._____

6. Although a few employees are hardworking and honest, most will try to take things from your business.
   6._____

7. A recovery plan is an important part of every risk management plan.
   7._____

8. Robbery is one of the risks of being open for business.
   8._____

9. To minimize losses from bad checks, you can establish a policy of accepting only checks drawn on in-state banks.
   9._____

10. Credit cards are seldom targets of theft.
    10._____

Multiple Choice

Directions   In the Answers column, write the letter that represents the word, or group of words, that correctly completes the statement.

Answers

1. Human risks (a) are caused by the actions of individuals, (b) are caused by acts of nature, (c) occur because of changes in business conditions, (d) all of these.
   1._____

2. Looking at all aspects of your business and determining the risks you face is called a(n) (a) recovery plan, (b) risk assumption, (c) insurance plan, (d) risk assessment.
   2._____

3. Installing electronic merchandise tags can help to (a) keep track of inventory, (b) increase sales, (c) reduce the risk of shoplifting, (d) decrease job-related injuries.
   3._____

4. Employee theft (a) cannot be prevented, (b) can devastate your business financially, (c) is often undetectable, (d) has little effect on profits.
   4._____

5. You transfer risk and protect yourself against financial losses from some risks by (a) installing deadbolts, (b) installing an alarm system, (c) installing surveillance cameras, (d) purchasing insurance.
   5._____

6. To limit losses in the event of a robbery, a business can (a) install dead-bolt locks, (b) hire a security guard, (c) transfer cash to a safe frequently, (d) encourage credit card use.
   6._____

7. An electronic credit authorizer is a machine that (a) allows a business owner to collect credit card fees, (b) checks to see if a credit card is valid, (c) identifies bad checks, (d) detects fraudulent drivers' licenses.
   7._____

8. The writer of a bounced check (a) cannot be identified, (b) has stolen credit cards and identification, (c) has insufficient funds in the checking account to cover the check, (d) has an out-of-state bank.
   8._____

Problem Solving

Directions   Answer the following questions in the space provided.

1. In the first column of the following table, list the methods that can prevent or reduce shoplifting. Then, rank the methods from 1 to 5 according to effectiveness, cost, and ease of implementation. A ranking of 1 should indicate the most effective, the least expensive, and the easiest to implement.

Method	Effectiveness	Cost	Ease of Implementation

2. In the first column of the following table, list the methods that can prevent or reduce employee theft. Then, rank the methods from 1 to 4 according to effectiveness, cost, and ease of implementation. A ranking of 1 should indicate the most effective, the least expensive, and the easiest to implement.

Method	Effectiveness	Cost	Ease of Implementation

Entrepreneurship: Ideas in Action, 5e, Student Edition

12.2 Insure Against Risks

True or False

Directions   Place a *T* for True or an *F* for False in the Answers column to show whether each of the following statements is true or false.

Answers

1. A payment made to an insurance company to cover the cost of insurance is a premium.   1._____

2. All risks are insurable.   2._____

3. A pure risk presents the chance of loss but no opportunity for gain.   3._____

4. The most important type of insurance you will need for your business is probably life insurance.   4._____

5. Liability insurance covers fire, robbery, storm damage, and floods.   5._____

6. Business interruption insurance covers the loss of income resulting from a fire or other catastrophe that disrupts the operation of the business.   6._____

7. Business owners buy life insurance so that their heirs have enough money to continue the business.   7._____

8. It is always a good idea to have extra insurance so every risk is more than covered.   8._____

9. To get the best price for insurance, compare policies from different insurance agents.   9._____

10. The first step in buying insurance is determining how much coverage you need.   10._____

Multiple Choice

Directions   In the Answers column, write the letter that represents the word, or group of words, that correctly completes the statement.

Answers

1. The classifications of risk are based on all of the following *except* the (a) result of the risk, (b) timing of the risk, (c) controllability of the risk, (d) insurability of the risk.   1._____

2. Which type of risk offers you the chance to gain as well as lose from the event or activity? (a) Speculative, (b) Pure, (c) Controllable, (d) Uncontrollable.   2._____

3. Which of the following would generally *not* be considered an uninsurable business risk? (a) Unpredictable economic factors, (b) Competitor's actions, (c) Fire, (d) None of these because all risks are insurable.   3._____

4. Property insurance usually does *not* cover losses due to (a) fire, (b) floods, (c) storm damage, (d) all of these.   4._____

5. The location of your business determines whether or not you need (a) property insurance, (b) life insurance, (c) flood insurance, (d) fire insurance.   5._____

6. This type of insurance covers your company's legal responsibility for the harm it may cause to others. (a) Life, (b) Liability, (c) Property, (d) Business interruption.   6._____

7. Your insurance agent should (a) be someone you trust, (b) work for many different insurance companies, (c) work for a single insurance company, (d) live near your business.   7._____

8. The second step in buying insurance is to (a) determine the kind of coverage you think you need, (b) select an insurance company, (c) determine how much coverage you need, (d) identify the kinds of risks you would like to insure against.   8._____

9. Uninsurable risks are tied to all of the following except (a) economic conditions, (b) technology changes, (c) competitors' actions, (d) robberies.   9._____

10. A business faces risk due to (a) an increase in local taxes, (b) poor management, (c) a decline in consumer demand, (d) all of these.   10._____

Problem Solving

Directions   Answer the following questions in the space provided.

1. The first column of the following table lists business risks. Complete the table by identifying the type of insurance that covers each risk.

Risk	Type of Insurance
Death of owner	
Lawsuit due to accident on premises	
Earthquake	
Robbery	
Lawsuit claiming that a defect in a product manufactured or sold caused bodily injury	
Contents owned by the renter inside a leased space are damaged	
Fire	
Flood	
Storm damage	
Extra expense of operating out of a temporary location after fire has destroyed the building	

2. Describe how to choose an insurance agent.

_____

_____

_____

_____

_____

3. Describe the process for determining insurance coverage for a business.

_____

_____

_____

_____

_____

Entrepreneurship: Ideas in Action, 5e, Student Edition

12.3 Other Risks

True or False

Directions   Place a *T* for True or an *F* for False in the Answers column to show whether each of the following statements is true or false.

Answers

1. Debtor-creditor relationships that involve extending credit can help increase a business's sales.   1._____

2. When one business allows another business to buy now and pay later, it is offering fair credit.   2._____

3. Consumer credit is offered in two basic forms: loans and trade credit.   3._____

4. An installment loan is paid back with interest in monthly equal amounts over a specified period of time.   4._____

5. Most credit cards are considered secured loans.   5._____

6. Employers, not employees, must pay the cost of workers' compensation insurance.   6._____

7. *All* injuries suffered on the job are covered by workers' compensation insurance.   7._____

8. It is the employee's, not the employer's, responsibility to file a workers' compensation claim.   8._____

9. Businesses in other countries may want to pay you with their country's currency.   9._____

10. Government agencies such as the International Trade Administration can assist companies that wish to do business overseas.   10._____

Multiple Choice

Directions   In the Answers column, write the letter that represents the word, or group of words, that correctly completes the statement.

Answers

1. When one business allows another business to buy now and pay later, it is offering (a) trade credit, (b) consumer credit, (c) an installment loan, (d) secured credit.   1._____

2. An unsecured loan is (a) granted based on the credit history of the individual, (b) a type of installment loan, (c) backed by collateral, (d) all of these.   2._____

3. Some things to consider in determining who is creditworthy include all of the following except the applicant's (a) previous credit history, (b) marital status, (c) employment record, (d) assets owned.   3._____

4. Uncollectible accounts (a) will not be a problem for a business that has established sound credit policies, (b) are an expense to a business, (c) increase net income, (d) occur only with secured loans.   4._____

5. The law that provides benefits to employees who have suffered work-related injuries or occupational diseases is the (a) Occupational Safety and Health Act, (b) Fair Labor Practices Act, (c) Equal Opportunity Act, (d) Federal Employees' Compensation Act.   5._____

6. Lost wage payments provided by workers' compensation are usually about ___ of the employee's income. (a) one-quarter, (b) 50 percent, (c) two-thirds, (d) 100 percent.   6._____

7. Which of the following injuries are not covered by workers' compensation insurance? (a) Self-inflicted injuries, (b) Injuries suffered during fights started by the injured, (c) Injuries suffered while disobeying employer policies, (d) All of these.   7._____

8. To minimize the risks of international business, you should (a) conduct business in only one foreign country, (b) never hire employees from the country you are targeting, (c) learn about the other country's culture, (d) all of these.   8._____

Problem Solving

Directions   Answer the following questions in the space provided.

1. Describe at least four challenges a business may face if it decides to do business in a foreign country.

_____

_____

_____

_____

_____

_____

_____

_____

_____

_____

2. Describe some strategies a business might take to deal with the risks you identified in Question 1.

_____

_____

_____

_____

_____

_____

_____

_____

_____

_____

3. Why would a business decide to accept credit cards issued by banks and credit card companies instead of issuing its own credit card?

_____

_____

_____

_____

_____

_____

_____

_____

_____

Entrepreneurship: Ideas in Action, 5e, Student Edition

Chapter 12 Assessment
Risk Management

Vocabulary Review

Directions   In each of the following sentences, the underlined term is not used correctly. In the space provided, rewrite the sentence so the term is used correctly.

1. Storms, fires, floods, and earthquakes are examples of <u>human risks,</u> or risks caused by the actions of individuals.

2. Businesses lose millions of dollars every year because of <u>shoplifting,</u> the act of purchasing goods using a stolen credit card.

3. Investing in the stock market is a good example of a <u>pure risk,</u> which presents the chance of loss but no opportunity for gain.

Fill-in-the-Blank

Directions   For each item below, determine the word(s) that best complete the sentence. Write the word(s) in the Answers column.

Answers

1. _____ is the possibility of some kind of loss.   1._____

2. A(n) _____ plan will enable you to get back to business as quickly as possible.   2._____

3. A(n) _____ check (or bad check) is returned to you by the bank because the customer's checking account has insufficient funds to cover the check amount.   3._____

4. A risk is an insurable risk if it is a(n) _____ risk faced by a large number of people and the amount of the loss can be predicted.   4._____

5. A payment made to an insurance company to cover the cost of insurance is a(n) _____.   5._____

6. To minimize losses from bad checks, a business may accept only checks drawn on _____ banks.   6._____

7. Many small and mid-sized businesses purchase a package known as a(n) _____ policy.   7._____

8. The person who sells you your insurance policy will be involved in processing your _____ if you ever need to collect on your policy.   8._____

9. Insurance agents earn _____ on the amount of coverage they sell.   9._____

10. _____ injuries result from performing the same activity repeatedly for long periods of time.   10._____

Problem Solving

Directions   Answer the following questions in the space provided.

1. Explain why some risks are uninsurable.

_____

_____

_____

_____

_____

_____

_____

_____

_____

_____

2. You plan to open a bookstore with a small cafe. List the types of risk you will face. Categorize them as human, natural, or economic and classify them as controllable/uncontrollable and insurable/uninsurable. For all insurable risks, list the type of insurance that you could purchase to protect against the risk.

_____

_____

_____

_____

_____

_____

_____

_____

_____

3. Suppose you plan to operate a comic book shop near a university. Will you offer customers credit? If not, explain your reasoning. If so, tell what kind of consumer credit you will offer and develop a credit policy.

_____

_____

_____

_____

_____

_____

_____

_____

_____

13.1 Growth Strategies

True or False

Directions   Place a *T* for True or an *F* for False in the Answers column to show whether each of the following statements is true or false.

Answers

1. To expand your business successfully, you will need to determine when and how to grow.   1._____

2. If you need more space even though your sales are not rising, it is time to expand.   2._____

3. If the condition of your business shows that you should expand, you should next analyze the economic climate that controls the business.   3._____

4. If a business grows too quickly, it may not have the resources, such as money, employees, or supplies, to support the growth.   4._____

5. Your expansion plan should include strategies for hiring managers and supervisors and for obtaining financing.   5._____

6. Market penetration is deciding to market a product or service in another town, city, or state.   6._____

7. Because increasing market share costs money, you may have smaller profits in the future even though you have a larger market share.   7._____

8. A prototype is a full-scale model of a new product.   8._____

9. In the maturity stage of the product life cycle, both sales and profits begin to drop rapidly.   9._____

10. One way to expand your business is to sell new products or services in addition to what you already offer.   10._____

Multiple Choice

Directions   In the Answers column, write the letter that represents the word, or group of words, that correctly completes the statement.

Answers

1. Determining when to expand depends on (a) the location of your business, (b) the condition of your business, (c) your product or service, (d) your fixed costs.   1._____

2. To analyze the economic climate that controls your business, you need to determine whether or not (a) demand for your product or service will remain strong, (b) your competitors plan to expand, (c) you can obtain financing, (d) all of these.   2._____

3. Your plan for expansion should include strategies for (a) assessing the economic condition of your industry, (b) increasing your advertising, (c) obtaining capital equipment, inventory, materials, and supplies, (d) locating your direct competition.   3._____

4. Increasing market share for a product or service within a given market in a given area is (a) geographic expansion, (b) market penetration, (c) market development, (d) product development.   4._____

5. You can increase your market share by (a) offering special deals to customers, (b) buying new equipment, (c) adding managers to your staff, (d) reducing your variable costs.   5._____

6. Sales peak and profits begin to decline during the ____ stage of the product life cycle. (a) introduction, (b) growth, (c) maturity, (d) decline.   6._____

7. The first step in new product development involves (a) idea development, (b) idea screening, (c) financial analysis, (d) product marketing.   7._____

8. During the ____?____ stage of the life cycle, sales peak and profits begin to decline. (a) decline, (b) maturity, (c) introduction, (d) growth.   8._____

Problem Solving

Directions   Answer the following questions in the space provided.

1. Briefly describe three different growth strategies.

   _____

   _____

   _____

   _____

   _____

   _____

2. List and describe stages in the product life cycle.

   _____

   _____

   _____

   _____

   _____

   _____

3. Why is it necessary for a business owner to prepare a plan before expanding her or his business?

   _____

   _____

   _____

   _____

   _____

   _____

4. The condition of a business and economic conditions indicate to the business owner that the business can expand. The business owner develops strategies for growth and writes an expansion plan. Why might the business owner decide at this point not to expand?

   _____

   _____

   _____

   _____

   _____

   _____

13.2 Ethical and Social Issues

True or False

Directions   Place a *T* for True or an *F* for False in the Answers column to show whether each of the following statements is true or false.

1. Even within the same culture, individuals develop different codes of ethics.   1._____

2. Ethics involves choosing between right and wrong.   2._____

3. Due to strict codes of ethics, businesses rarely face ethical dilemmas.   3._____

4. Employees will not act ethically unless they see the business owner acting in an ethical manner.   4._____

5. You should create a code of ethics as soon as you begin your business.   5._____

6. One of your responsibilities to customers is to treat all personal information confidentially.   6._____

7. To make sure you maintain good relationships with suppliers, you should do what they suggest.   7._____

8. If you change suppliers, you should not give a reason for your decision.   8._____

9. Business owners can contribute to their community by donating money and goods or services.   9._____

10. An entrepreneur has an obligation to do as little harm as possible to the environment.   10._____

Multiple Choice

Directions   In the Answers column, write the letter that represents the word, or group of words, that correctly completes the statement.

1. Ethics is the study of (a) honesty, (b) different cultures, (c) moral choices and values, (d) business behavior.   1._____

2. Paying bribes is an accepted business practice (a) in some cultures, (b) in all countries, (c) in most of the United States, (d) except where prohibited by law.   2._____

3. If you follow ethical business practices, (a) you will decrease profits, (b) suppliers will charge you higher prices, (c) customers may be more willing to do business with you, (d) you will have difficulty hiring qualified employees.   3._____

4. Your employees are more likely to act ethically if (a) they act without thinking, (b) your business requires a license, (c) they see you acting in an ethical manner, (d) they are well paid.   4._____

5. To write an effective code of ethics for your business, you should (a) take a course in ethics, (b) ask a lawyer for guidelines to follow, (c) think about ethical dilemmas that may arise and come up with solutions for dealing with them, (d) all of these.   5._____

6. When dealing with customers, you should (a) treat all customers with respect, (b) exaggerate the merits of your products or services, (c) take advantage of an unknowledgeable customer, (d) let them know if your business is in financial trouble.   6._____

7. A business owner should never conceal losses from (a) customers, (b) competitors, (c) investors, (d) all of these.   7._____

8. Federal laws concerning clean air and water are enforced by the (a) Environmental Protection Department, (b) Federal Trade Commission, (c) Environmental Protection Agency, (d) Consumer Product Safety Commission.   8._____

Problem Solving

Directions   Answer the following questions in the space provided.

1. Explain how culture affects ethical behavior.

   _____

   _____

   _____

   _____

2. Do consumers sometimes demand higher codes of ethics from businesses than from themselves? Explain your answer.

   _____

   _____

   _____

   _____

3. What will happen to a business that does not meet its responsibilities to its customers?

   _____

   _____

   _____

   _____

4. What will happen to a business that does not meet its responsibilities to its suppliers?

   _____

   _____

   _____

   _____

5. What will happen to a business that does not meet its responsibilities to its community?

   _____

   _____

   _____

   _____

Entrepreneurship: Ideas in Action, 5e, Student Edition

13.3 Global Trends and Opportunities

True or False

Directions   Place a *T* for True or an *F* for False in the Answers column to show whether each of the following statements is true or false.

Answers

1. Products that are made and sold in the United States are considered exports.

    1. _____

2. To export their goods or services, businesses may hire special sales representatives or use commissioned agents to find foreign buyers.

    2. _____

3. Entrepreneurs may use imported parts to manufacture their own products.

    3. _____

4. A benefit of competing globally is that you will widen your customer base.

    4. _____

5. Every business can be successful in the global marketplace.

    5. _____

6. In analyzing the international market, you will have to consider political, economic, social, and cultural issues.

    6. _____

7. An international business plan that is an extension of your original business plan can be helpful when considering international expansion.

    7. _____

8. Trade protections are established by governments to keep foreign businesses from competing with domestic producers.

    8. _____

9. A standard of quality an exported product must meet before it can be sent to another country is a qualitative restriction.

    9. _____

10. The North American Free Trade Agreement removed most trade barriers among Mexico, Canada, and the United States.

    10. _____

Multiple Choice

Directions   In the Answers column, write the letter that represents the word, or group of words, that correctly completes the statement.

Answers

1. Exporting goods by finding foreign buyers or distributors and then shipping your product to them (a) is indirect exporting, (b) requires using commissioned agents, (c) is direct exporting, (d) is a benefit of global competition.

    1. _____

2. Exporting through commissioned agents is (a) direct exporting, (b) indirect exporting, (c) not recommended for small businesses, (d) not cost-effective.

    2. _____

3. Entrepreneurs may import products because (a) consumers are attracted by their low price, (b) they use them to manufacture their products, (c) consumers are attracted by their high quality, (d) all of these.

    3. _____

4. Selling internationally over the Internet is another way to get involved in (a) trade embargos, (b) new markets, (c) direct exporting, (d) international travel.

    4. _____

5. Before you trade internationally, you should write an international business plan that indicates (a) when you plan to begin exporting products, (b) what costs you expect to have, (c) how you will learn about the culture, (d) who your competitors will be.

    5. _____

6. A limit on the amount of a product that can be imported into a country over a particular period of time is a (a) quota, (b) markup, (c) tariff, (d) qualitative restriction.

    6. _____

7. A tax on imports is a (a) quota, (b) markup, (c) tariff, (d) qualitative restriction.

    7. _____

8. To help U.S. businesses operate in foreign markets, the federal government offers programs in (a) export counseling, (b) export financing, (c) technical assistance, (d) all of these.

    8. _____

Problem Solving

Directions   Answer the following questions in the space provided.

1. A business may get involved in international trade via direct exporting, indirect exporting, or the World Wide Web. Which exporting method do you think is easiest? Which is the riskiest? Which requires the most knowledge about a foreign country? Explain your responses.

_____

_____

_____

_____

_____

_____

_____

_____

2. As an exporter, which type of trade barrier do you think would be easiest to deal with?

_____

_____

_____

_____

_____

_____

_____

3. All trade barriers protect domestic producers. Why would a government choose one trade barrier over another?

_____

_____

_____

_____

_____

_____

_____

Chapter 13 Assessment
Management for the Future

Vocabulary Review

Directions In the Answers column, write the letter that represents the word, or group of words, that correctly completes the statement.

Answers

1. Increasing market share for a product or service within a given market in a given area
2. The application of the principles of right and wrong to issues that come up in the workplace
3. The stages a product goes through from the time it is introduced to when it is no longer sold
4. A standard of quality an imported product must meet before it can be sold
5. A limit on the amount of a product that can be imported into a country over a particular period of time
6. A set of standards or rules that outlines the ethical behavior demanded by an individual, a business, or a culture
7. Products and services that are brought in from another country to be sold
8. Products and services that are produced in one country and sent to another country to be sold
9. Methods for keeping foreign businesses from competing with domestic producers

a. business ethics
b. code of ethics
c. exports
d. imports
e. market penetration
f. product life cycle
g. qualitative restriction
h. quota
i. trade barriers

1._____
2._____
3._____
4._____
5._____
6._____
7._____
8._____
9._____

Fill-in-the-Blank

Directions For each item below, determine the word(s) that best complete the sentence. Write the word(s) in the Answers column.

Answers

1. Market _____ is a strategy for expanding the target market of a business
2. A tariff is a tax on _____.
3. Ethics is the study of moral choices and _____.
4. A prototype is a full-scale _____ of a new product.
5. In the growth stage of the product life cycle, a product will attract more customers and sales begin to_____.
6. Businesses should conserve _____ resources, such as coal and oil, by using them efficiently.
7. _____ are a business's most important asset, and they need to be treated ethically.
8. Some businesses use commissioned agents who act as _____ to find foreign buyers for products and services.
9. Participating in the global marketplace can _____ a business's dependence on current markets and suppliers.
10. For _____ exporting, a business may need to hire salespeople who live in or travel to the foreign countries.

1._____
2._____
3._____
4._____
5._____
6._____
7._____
8._____
9._____
10._____

Problem Solving

Directions   Answer the following questions in the space provided.

1. In the table below, identify the four stages of the product life cycle and name a currently available product that fits into each stage.

Life Cycle Stage	Product Example

2. Business owners have a responsibility to contribute to their communities. Provide an example of a business in your area that has contributed to the community in some way.

_____

_____

_____

_____

_____

_____

_____

3. Should a business code of ethics be different from a personal code of ethics? Explain your answer.

_____

_____

_____

_____

_____

_____

_____

4. How does it benefit a business to respect the environment?

_____

_____

_____

_____

_____

_____